U. S. SECRET
BRITISH MOST SECRET

RETURN TO JOINT CHIEFS OF STAFF
R&RA SECTION, ROOM 2-C-934
THE PENTAGON

PROCEEDINGS

OF THE

AMERICAN - BRITISH JOINT CHIEFS OF STAFF CONFERENCES

HELD IN WASHINGTON, D. C.

ON TWELVE OCCASIONS

BETWEEN DECEMBER 24, 1941 AND JANUARY 14, 1942

IN TWO PARTS

PART I - MINUTES OF THE CONFERENCES

PART II - APPROVED DOCUMENTS

DECLASSIFIED BY:
JCS-CCS DECLASSIFICATION
WORKING GROUP
DATE 26 Sep 1973

J.C.S. FILE COPY

Published by Books Express Publishing
Copyright © Books Express, 2011
ISBN 978-1-780393-95-7

Books Express publications are available from all good retail and online booksellers. For publishing proposals and direct ordering please contact us at: info@books-express.com

U. S. SECRET
BRITISH MOST SECRET

PART I

MINUTES OF CONFERENCES

NOTE

The Minutes of each Conference with Annexes are considered as Separate Documents and the pages are numbered accordingly. The titles are abbreviated by the symbols JCCSs 1 to 12 inclusive.

U. S. SECRET
BRITISH MOST SECRET

LIST OF PAPERS

JCCSs-1   DECEMBER 24, 1941

SUBJECTS DISCUSSED

1. Defense of the British Isles.
2. Heavy Bombers.
3. Relief of British Troops in Northern Ireland and Iceland.
4. Greenland.
5. Anti-submarine Measures and Escorts.
6. Portuguese and Spanish Islands in the Atlantic.
7. Occupation of Africa.
8. Brazil.
9. The Curacao-Aruba Area.
10. The Pacific Area.
11. Bombardment of Japan.
12. Russian Situation.
13. Spain and Portugal.
14. Airplane Carriers.
15. PBY's for the British
16. British Crews for American Ships.
17. Guns for Merchant Ships.
18. Naval Dispositions in the Atlantic.
19. Priorities in Expeditions.
20. West Africa.
21. British Chiefs of Staff Memorandum (Annex 1)
22. British Estimate of Attack on West Coast of North America.

ANNEX 1:   American-British Strategy.

   British WW-1 (U.S. Revised)

ANNEX 2:   Probable Maximum Scale of Enemy Attack on West Coast of North America.

   Appendix A to ANNEX 2:   Distance Chart.

U. S. SECRET
BRITISH MOST SECRET

JCCSs-2   DECEMBER 25, 1941

SUBJECTS DISCUSSED

1. Program of Planning (Joint Planning Committee).
2. Disposition of the MOUNT VERNON.
3. Diversion of Reinforcements (intended for the Philippines).
4. Unified Command.
5. Disposition of Forces Destined for the Far East.

ANNEX 1:   Memorandum for the President: Utilization of United States Forces in Australia.

U. S. SECRET
BRITISH MOST SECRET

JCCSs-3   DECEMBER 26, 1941

SUBJECTS DISCUSSED

1. Priorities for United States and United Kingdom Overseas Expeditions in the Atlantic Ocean. (ABC-4/1).
2. Northwest Africa Project.

ANNEX 1: Priorities for United States and United Kingdom Overseas Expeditions in the Atlantic Ocean. (Report by Joint Planning Committee)

    U.S. Serial ABC-4/1
    British Serial WW (J.P.C.) 1

ANNEX 2: Project - Gymnast. (Report by Joint Planning Committee)

    U.S. Serial ABC-4/2
    British Serial WW (J.P.C.) 2

U. S. SECRET
BRITISH MOST SECRET

JCCSs-4   DECEMBER 27, 1941

SUBJECTS DISCUSSED

1. ABC-4/1 -- Priorities for United States - United Kingdom Expeditions in the Atlantic Ocean.
2. ABC-4/2 -- Plan for Expedition to Northwest Africa.
3. American - British Strategy.
4. Program of Work of the Joint Planning Committee.
5. Unity of Command.
6. Utilization of the United States Transports now being used in the Indian Ocean.

ANNEX 1:   Proposed Draft of Instructions to the Supreme Commander, Southwestern Pacific Theater.
ABC-4, C/S USA.

U. S. SECRET
BRITISH MOST SECRET

JCCSs-5   DECEMBER 29, 1941

SUBJECTS DISCUSSED

1. Priorities for United States and United Kingdom Overseas Expeditions in the Atlantic Ocean.
2. American-British Strategy (British WW-1). (Action deferred).
3. Northwest Africa Project (U.S. ABC-4/2),
                             (British WW (J.P.C.) 2).
                                                   (Action deferred).
4. Supporting Measures for the Southwest Pacific.
                             (U.S. ABC-4/3),
                             (British WW (J.P.C.) 3).
                                                   (Action deferred).
5. Unity of Command in the Southwestern Pacific Theater.
6. Proposed Communication to Generalissimo Chiang Kai-Shek.

ANNEX 1: Priorities for United States and United Kingdom Overseas Expeditions in the Atlantic Ocean.   (Report by Joint Planning Committee)

    ABC-4/1   APPROVED DOCUMENT
    British WW-5
    British WW (J.P.C.) 1

ANNEX 2: Proposed Method of Handling Matters Concerning the Southwest Pacific Theater.

ANNEX 3: Memorandum for the President: Draft of Message to Generalissimo Chiang Kai-Shek.

U. S. SECRET
BRITISH MOST SECRET

JCCSs-6   DECEMBER 30, 1941

SUBJECTS DISCUSSED

1. Higher Direction of War in the ABDA Area.
2. Draft Directive to the Supreme Commander in the ABDA Area.
3. Next Meeting, to consider:

   a. Northwest Africa Project (U.S. ABC-4/2),
   (British WW (J.P.C.) 2)

   b. Supporting Measures for the Southwestern Pacific
   (U.S. ABC-4/3),
   (British WW (J.P.C.) 3)

ANNEX 1: Letter (Mr. Hopkins to Admiral Stark) enclosing Proposed Method of Handling Matters concerning the Southwest Pacific Theater.

ANNEX 2: In Two Parts:

   Part I - Memorandum for the President: Higher Direction of War in the ABDA Area.

   Part II - Higher Direction of War in the ABDA Area.

ANNEX 3: Draft Directive to the Supreme Commander in the ABDA Area.

   U.S. ABC-4/5
   British WW-3

   Annex 1 to ANNEX 3: Boundaries of ABDA Area.

   Annex 2 to ANNEX 3: Higher Direction of War in the ABDA Area.

U. S. SECRET
BRITISH MOST SECRET

JCCSs-7   DECEMBER 31, 1941

SUBJECTS DISCUSSED

1. Withdrawal of United States Marines from Iceland.
2. American-British Strategy.
3. Supporting Measures for the Southwest Pacific.
4. Northwest Africa Project.
5. Relief of the British Garrison in Northern Ireland.
6. Draft Directive to the Supreme Commander in the ABDA Area.
7. Proposed Tasks for the Joint Planning Committee.
8. Naval Dispositions.

ANNEX 1:   American-British Grand Strategy.

        U.S. ABC-4/CS 1   APPROVED DOCUMENT
        British WW-1 (Final)

ANNEX 2:   Supporting Measures for the Southwest Pacific (the Far East Area and Adjacent Regions) until Establishment of Unified Command. (Approved Report of Joint Planning Committee)

        U.S. ABC-4/3   APPROVED DOCUMENT
        British WW-4
        British Serial WW (J.P.C.) 3

        Annex I to ANNEX 2:   Chart: Far East Forces and Reinforcements Therefor, United States.

        Annex II to ANNEX 2: Chart: Far East Forces and Reinforcements Therefor, British Commonwealth.

        Annex III to ANNEX 2: Chart: Forces Now in the Far East -- Dutch and Australian.

ANNEX 3:   Draft Directive to the Supreme Commander in the ABDA Area.

        U.S. ABC-4/5 (Final)
        British WW-3

        Annex 1 to ANNEX 3:   Boundaries of ABDA Area.

        Annex 2 to ANNEX 3:   Higher Direction of War in the ABDA Area.

ANNEX 4:   Proposed Tasks for the Joint Planning Committee.

        U.S. ABC-4/4 (Final)   APPROVED DOCUMENT
        British WW (J.P.C.) 4

U. S. SECRET
BRITISH MOST SECRET

JCCSs-8   JANUARY 10, 1942

<u>SUBJECTS DISCUSSED</u>

    1. Super-Gymnast.
    2. Directive for the Supreme Commander of the ABDA Area -- Attitude of the Dutch.
    3. Procedure for the Assumption of Command by General Wavell.
    4. Immediate Assistance to China.
    5. Post-Arcadia Collaboration.

ANNEX 1: <u>Directive to the Supreme Commander in the ABDA Area (Approved by the President and the Prime Minister)</u>.

    U.S. ABC-4/5 (Approved)   <u>APPROVED DOCUMENT</u>
    British WW-6
    (Supersedes ABC-4/5, WW-3, Final, Annex 3 to JCCSs-7)

    <u>Annex 1 to ANNEX 1</u>: <u>Boundaries of ABDA Area</u>.

    <u>Annex 2 to ANNEX 1</u>: <u>Higher Direction of War in the ABDA Area</u>.

ANNEX 2: <u>Procedure for Assumption of Command by General Wavell</u>.

    U.S. ABC-4/CS 3   <u>APPROVED DOCUMENT</u>
    British WW-9 (Revised)

    <u>Annex A to ANNEX 2</u>: <u>Draft Telegram from His Majesty's Government to United States, The Netherlands, Australia, New Zealand, China, India</u>.

    <u>Annex B to ANNEX 2</u>: <u>Draft Telegram from His Majesty's Government to General Wavell</u>.

    <u>Annex C to ANNEX 2</u>: <u>Draft Telegram from British Chiefs of Staff to Chiefs of Staff Committee in London</u>.

ANNEX 3: <u>Immediate Assistance to China</u>. (Approved Joint Planning Committee Report)

    U.S. ABC-4/9   <u>APPROVED DOCUMENT</u>
    British WW-10
    British Serial WW (J.P.C.) 9

ANNEX 4: <u>Post-Arcadia Collaboration</u>.
    British WW-8.

U. S. SECRET
BRITISH MOST SECRET

JCCSs-9   JANUARY 11, 1942

SUBJECTS DISCUSSED

1. Establishment of Command in the ABDA Area.
2. Situation in the ABDA Area.
3. Establishment of United States forces in Northern Ireland.
    (ABC-4/7, WW (J.P.C.) 7).
4. Defense of Island Bases between Hawaii and Australia.
    (ABC-4/8, WW (J.P.C.) 8).
5. Inclusion of Port Darwin in the ABDA Area.

ANNEX 1:   Establishment of United States Forces in North Ireland.

        U.S. Serial ABC-4/7   APPROVED DOCUMENT
        British Serial WW-12
        British Serial WW (J.P.C.) 7

U. S. SECRET
BRITISH MOST SECRET

JCCSs-10   JANUARY 12, 1942

SUBJECTS DISCUSSED

1. Shipping for United States Reinforcements for the Far East.
2. Defense of Island Bases between Hawaii and Australia.
   (ABC-4/8, WW (J.P.C.) 8).

ANNEX 1:   Memorandum of Proposed Shipping Adjustments.

ANNEX 2:   Defense of Island Bases between Hawaii and Australia.

        U.S. Serial ABC-4/8   APPROVED DOCUMENT
        British Serial WW-13
        British Serial WW (J.P.C.) 8

        Annex to ANNEX 2:   Table showing Defense of Island Bases between Hawaii and Australia.

U. S. SECRET
BRITISH MOST SECRET

JCCSs-11   JANUARY 13, 1942

SUBJECTS DISCUSSED

1. Post-Arcadia Collaboration
2. Movements and Projects in the Atlantic Theater - First Half of 1942.
3. Operation Super-Gymnast.

ANNEX 1: Post-Arcadia Collaboration.

    British WW-8.

    Minute to ANNEX 1:   Body to Allocate Equipment.

ANNEX 2: Movements and Projects in the Atlantic Theater -- First Half of 1942.

    U.S. ABC-4/6   APPROVED DOCUMENT
    British WW-14
    British Serial WW (J.P.C.) 6.

U. S. SECRET
BRITISH MOST SECRET

JCCSs-12   JANUARY 14, 1942

SUBJECTS DISCUSSED

1. Move of United States Reinforcements to the Far East.
2. Super-Gymnast.
3. Post-Arcadia Collaboration.

ANNEX 1:   Operation Super-Gymnast.

        U.S. ABC-4/2A   APPROVED DOCUMENT
        British WW-17
        British WW (J.P.C.) 2A.

ANNEX 2:   Post-Arcadia Collaboration.

        U.S. ABC-4/CS 4   APPROVED DOCUMENT
        British WW-16

U. S. SECRET
BRITISH MOST SECRET

ABC-4
JCCSs-1

December 24, 1941.

THE CHIEFS OF STAFF CONFERENCE

FEDERAL RESERVE BUILDING

WASHINGTON, D. C.

10:30 A.M., DECEMBER 24, 1941

Present

British Officers

    Admiral of the Fleet, Sir Dudley Pound, First Sea Lord and Chief of Naval Staff
    Field Marshal Sir John Dill
    Air Chief Marshal Sir Charles Portal, Chief of Air Staff
    Admiral Sir Charles Little, Joint Staff Mission
    Lieut. General Sir Colville Wemyss, Joint Staff Mission
    Air Marshal A. T. Harris, Joint Staff Mission

U. S. Naval Officers

    Admiral H. R. Stark, Chief of Naval Operations
    Admiral E. J. King, Commander-in-Chief, U. S. Fleet
    Rear Admiral W. R. Sexton, President of the General Board
    Rear Admiral F. J. Horne, Assistant Chief of Naval Operations
    Rear Admiral J. H. Towers, Chief, Bureau of Aeronautics
    Rear Admiral R. K. Turner, Director, War Plans Division
    Major General Thomas Holcomb, Commandant, U. S. Marine Corps

U. S. Army Officers

    General George C. Marshall, Commanding General of the Field Forces and Chief of Staff, U. S. Army
    Lieut. General H. H. Arnold, Chief of Army Air Forces and Deputy Chief of Staff, U. S. Army
    Brigadier General L. T. Gerow, Chief of War Plans Division

U. S. SECRET
BRITISH MOST SECRET

Joint Secretaries

    Brigadier L. C. Hollis, R. M.
    Colonel E. I. C. Jacob
    Commander Coleridge, R. N.
    Captain J. L. McCrea, Aide to Chief of Naval Operations, U. S. Navy
    Lieut. Colonel R. M. Robinett, G-2, General Headquarters, U.S.A.
    Major W. T. Sexton, Asst. Secretary, War Department General Staff

The substance of the conference consisted of informal discussions of various points which had been brought up at a conference the previous evening at the White House, at which the President and Mr. Winston Churchill had been present.

    1.   DEFENSE OF THE BRITISH ISLES. -

ADMIRAL STARK opened the discussion with the remark that he believed it apparent to all that the British Isles was the fortress which must be protected at all cost, and that in this there was no serious difference of opinion. He remarked that he was wondering as to the effectiveness of the United Kingdom defenses as regards invasion from the Continent, remarking that at least two Marine Corps observers, after an inspection of the Island defenses, had come to the conclusion that they left much to be desired. ADMIRAL STARK stated that the comments of these officers would be transmitted to the British for such use as they might care to make of them.

MARSHAL DILL remarked that the defenses were constantly being improved.

ADMIRAL POUND welcomed Admiral Stark's proposal.

    2.   HEAVY BOMBERS. -

ADMIRAL STARK made the point that in the future, heavy bombers sent to Great Britain would be manned by American crews; that some would be sent as units.

AIR CHIEF MARSHAL PORTAL remarked that this had not been the original agreement. GENERAL ARNOLD stated that the R.A.F. was not to be deprived of any heavy bombers previously agreed to, but that units would be sent in addition. Details to be worked out later.

GENERAL MARSHALL remarked that Mr. Churchill had mentioned that the presence of American bombers, even in small numbers, in England would have an important influence on the French and the Germans.

U. S. SECRET
BRITISH MOST SECRET

3. RELIEF OF BRITISH TROOPS IN NORTHERN IRELAND AND ICELAND. -

THE PRIME MINISTER had requested that three British divisions in Northern Ireland be relieved at the earliest practicable date.

MARSHAL DILL remarked that it was his understanding that the relieving force was to consist of three divisions plus one armored division. GENERAL MARSHALL agreed. ADMIRAL POUND asked at what time the troops in Ireland could be relieved. GENERAL MARSHALL replied that the troops are available now; the question is the availability of tonnage.

ADMIRAL POUND asked with whom he could get in touch on the tonnage matter, and was told that his representatives should see Colonel Gross of the G-4 Division, War Department General Staff.

ADMIRAL STARK stated that the United States was ready to take over the defense of Iceland, following which, however, base facilities would still be available to Great Britain. He also stated that the Marines in Iceland are an important element of the United States amphibious force, and that it was desired that they be relieved prior to beginning the relief of the British troops there.

MARSHAL DILL remarked that this would have to be worked out, and asked when the relief of the British could be accomplished. GENERAL GEROW replied that it could be completed by March, 1942.

ADMIRAL STARK added that the whole question of relief was largely a matter of shipping, and added that United States production is behind in antiaircraft weapons, and that the British might be able to help out.

THE CONFERENCE agreed that the programs for these reliefs should be studied by the Joint Committee.

4. GREENLAND. -

ADMIRAL STARK brought up the question of Greenland and asked General Arnold the status of air fields there. GENERAL ARNOLD stated that the United States now has a small force in Greenland; that two fields are projected; one field is ready now, but in the fog belt; another field, farther to the north, will be ready very soon. He stated that Greenland will be used essentially as a staging area between the United States and Europe. He added that he could furnish more details later.

5. ANTI-SUBMARINE MEASURES AND ESCORTS. -

ADMIRAL STARK stated that these would continue, in collaboration with the British; that the Prime Minister had mentioned the possibility of

U. S. SECRET
BRITISH MOST SECRET

getting additional United States destroyers. ADMIRAL STARK continued, "We just don't have any destroyers to spare, and in fact have far fewer than we require for our own needs." The construction program, he stated, was farthest behind in destroyers, battleships, and patrol vessels. He said that the situation along American seacoasts, with regard to the need for corvettes and other small patrol craft, is critical. In fact, it is desired that the British lend to the United States any available vessels suitable for coastal patrol work.

ADMIRAL POUND then suggested that the whole question of general Naval dispositions of the two Navies be discussed.

6. PORTUGUESE AND SPANISH ISLANDS IN THE ATLANTIC. -

ADMIRAL STARK asked Admiral Pound what importance he attached to the Azores. ADMIRAL POUND stated that the British attached tremendous importance to these Islands, particularly if Gibralter should become untenable. He said, "We need the Azores very much; they have great importance from every point of view." ADMIRAL POUND went on to say that the Canaries also are important; that they might be invited to go in there.

ADMIRAL STARK then asked what importance the British attach to the Cape Verde Islands. ADMIRAL POUND replied that it was only a question of denying them to the enemy, rather than their actual use by the British. ADMIRAL KING then remarked that United States interest in the Cape Verde Islands is strategic, because of their location between Dakar and Brazil. He went on to say that "we can not do all these things"; the British should take the responsibility for the Azores, and the United States for the Cape Verde Islands.

ADMIRAL STARK suggested that further study be given to this question, to which ADMIRAL POUND agreed.

7. OCCUPATION OF AFRICA. -

ADMIRAL STARK said that he felt it undesirable for the United States to consider sending troops to Egypt or Libya. If the British can continue there and clean up, it would automatically protect Dakar, and at the same time Iran and Iraq would be of no great concern. So far as West Africa is concerned, the United States should fall in line with British action.

GENERAL MARSHALL read notes taken from a memorandum made at the White House conference yesterday, to the effect that if the British should reach Tunis there was the possibility of a French invitation to occupy North Africa.

U. S. SECRET
BRITISH MOST SECRET

      MARSHAL DILL pointed out that the British had available to move on 23 days' notice, an expeditionary force of 55,000 men which could be reinforced from Malta; that the Prime Minister had thought that if this occasion arose, it would be desirable for United States forces to land in Morocco, possibly to precede the British.

      GENERAL MARSHALL said that at the present time a Corps Commander is planning an expedition to Africa which would include an emphibious corps. That this would be a task force, ready for any action that might present itself; and that if an opportunity existed to occupy North Africa without difficulty, the United States should take advantage of it. That United States troops for this purpose are available, but that there is a shortage in anti-aircraft guns, .50 caliber ammunition and 37 mm. ammunition for both antiaircraft and anti-tank guns; also a shortage of planes. However, if the initial move could be made without fighting, the United States has already organized a sufficient number of squadrons to take care of the operation; that time is of greatest importance, and that while the American force could not complete its movement within 23 days, it could within approximately 30 days at the earliest, contingent on the availability of tonnage.

      ADMIRAL KING asked as to the possibility of furnishing an American token force, such as a regiment.

      GENERAL MARSHALL said that a token force as part of the British forces would be feasible, but that he could not put a lone regiment on the coast of Africa. The question was asked as to whether the Marines now in Iceland could be ready for this move. GENERAL HOLCOMB agreed that they could be.

      THE CONFERENCE agreed that this question should be studied by the Joint Planning Committee.

    8.   BRAZIL. -

      ADMIRAL KING said that the political situation in Brazil made the United States Marine-Naval position of a "touch and go" nature; that the Germans are well organized in Brazil and have followers among important members of the Government. If it becomes necessary to occupy Brazil, such a move might meet with armed resistance

      GENERAL MARSHALL said that after prolonged negotiations, the United States has been able to place only a small number of unarmed Marines in Brazil.

    9.   THE CURACAO-ARUBA AREA. -

      ADMIRAL STARK brought up the question of the critical situation in the Curacao-Aruba area with respect to Allied oil supply, pointing out

U. S. SECRET
BRITISH MOST SECRET

that 95% of the oil used on the eastern coast comes from that area; and that one-half of the Lend-Lease oil for Britain comes from that area. He stated that the troops on these Islands should be placed on the strictest alert; that time was of the greatest importance; and suggested that the British Chiefs of Staff do everything they could with their own authorities in London to expedite American entry into these Islands, particularly aviation units.

ADMIRAL POUND agreed to take the matter up that afternoon.

10. PACIFIC AREA. -

ADMIRAL STARK listed the joint aims in the Pacific, as follows:
    Protection of the Burma Road
    Aid to China
    Aid to the Netherlands East Indies
    To hold Singapore
    To hold the Philippine Islands
    Use of Australia as a base.

ADMIRAL STARK then reviewed the Naval situation in the Far East as pertains to the Asiatic Fleet. GENERAL MARSHALL reviewed the arrangements which had been made to get planes to the Philippines, not only from Australia, but by convoys; also by flying by way of the eastern route. GENERAL MARSHALL stated that the critical feature of assistance to the Philippines from Australia was the existence of fields in Borneo; and that the present issue is to elaborate our plans for building up bases in Australia.

ADMIRAL POUND then reviewed what ships the British Navy has around Singapore.

The question was asked MARSHAL DILL as to his opinion of the situation at Singapore, to which he replied that, with reinforcements, the British would be able to hold Johore State.

11. BOMBARDMENT OF JAPAN. -

ADMIRAL STARK asked as to the situation in China for air fields to be used as bases for bombing attacks against Japan.

GENERAL ARNOLD stated that General Brett had written for air transport planes for use in reconnaissance work and for supply. He stated that no bombing operations should be undertaken against Japan unless they are strong enough to create substantial damage; that the minimum number of bombers should be 50; that unsustained attacks would only tend to solidify the Japanese people.

U. S. SECRET
BRITISH MOST SECRET

12. RUSSIAN SITUATION.-

It was stated that it is not practicable at this time for Russia to begin operations in the Far East, as it might jeopardize her efforts in the west, and that Stalin should not be urged. The Prime Minister had quoted Stalin as saying that Russia was not ready to enter the war in the Far East now, but perhaps would be able do so in the spring.

13. SPAIN AND PORTUGAL.-

ADMIRAL STARK brought up the question of German intentions in the Iberian Peninsula, and expressed fear of German action through that area. He asked Admiral Pound for his views, who replied that British Joint Intelligence reports no signs of concentration of German troops in the south of France. ADMIRAL STARK remarked that, nevertheless, everyone should be on guard. He then asked Marshal Dill as to the significance of the change in the German high command. MARSHAL DILL stated that it probably concerned a difference of opinion on future operations.

14. AIRPLANE CARRIERS.-

ADMIRAL STARK said that the United States situation with respect to airplane carriers was very bad, and that while the Navy was making plans to convert passenger ships and tankers into ariplane carriers, in view of possible troop transport requirements, he had agreed to discuss proposed conversions with General Marshall. ADMIRAL STARK stated that with respect to flying boats for the British, the situation was such that the United States could not furnish any.

15. P.B.Y's FOR THE BRITISH.-

The conversation then was directed to the supply of heavy bombers and P.B.Y's for the British. ADMIRAL TOWERS remarked that our present production of P.B.Y's was 46 per month, and that this was being stepped up to 150 of all types. ADMIRAL KING pointed out that the bottleneck was really one of personnel rather than anything else. ADMIRAL STARK remarked that all possible help has been given the British in the matter of aircraft. REAR ADMIRAL TOWERS pointed out that the four-engine bomber program can not but interfere with the Naval aircraft progress for at least the next eight months. To emphasize his statement, he remarked that some American Naval aircraft factories, because of the four-engine bomber program, can only obtain material enough for an eight hour, five-day week.

16. BRITISH CREWS FOR AMERICAN SHIPS.-

ADMIRAL STARK said that available personnel for American merchant ships is so limited that he would like the British to consider the possibility of having British crews man American ships. ADMIRAL POUND said the

U. S. SECRET
BRITISH MOST SECRET

matter was questionable and that it should be discussed with Admiral Little.

17. GUNS FOR MERCHANT SHIPS. -

The question of guns for American ships was brought up. The United States Navy has furnished the British with 400 guns for arming merchant vessels. ADMIRAL STARK inquired if any of these could be returned, as there was a shortage.

ADMIRAL POUND stated that he would have the matter examined and do the best he could to meet the American requirements, which were to be made known to him.

18. NAVAL DISPOSITIONS IN THE ATLANTIC. -

ADMIRAL STARK proposed that the British take over capital ship responsibility in the Atlantic, and listed fleet elements that would be required in that ocean.

19. PRIORITIES IN EXPEDITIONS. -

GENERAL MARSHALL brought up the question of priorities in expeditions, and asked Marshal Dill if he had set up any such priorities. MARSHAL DILL said that the priorities were in the following order:
>Africa
>Iceland
>North Ireland.

GENERAL MARSHALL then asked if the French do not invite an occupation, what disposition will be made of the expeditionary force of 55,000.

MARSHAL DILL said that if the Germans go through Spain, the British hope to take the Canaries, whether invited or not.

GENERAL MARSHALL then asked how many troops would be required, and MARSHAL DILL replied only a small force of a few battalions. The British do not want any more than that down there. The question was then asked, if the British take the offensive and occupy the Canary Islands, what cooperation would be expected of the United States. ADMIRAL POUND, by nodded consent, indicated that the United States should take action in the Cape Verde Islands.

20. WEST AFRICA. -

GENERAL MARSHALL brought up the question of what was to be done at Freetown and Bathurst. This question was not settled.

U. S. SECRET
BRITISH MOST SECRET

ADMIRAL POUND then asked about Dakar. ADMIRAL TURNER stated that the United States is getting up a plan for its occupation.

ADMIRAL STARK asked Marshal Dill if he agreed that Dakar could be taken by direct attack. MARSHAL DILL stated that it could be done.

21. BRITISH CHIEFS OF STAFF MEMORANDUM. -

ADMIRAL POUND then read a memorandum signed by the British Chiefs of Staff, which was amended in minor points. (See Annex 1 for Revised Version). During the discussion, the following points were brought out:

MARSHAL DILL was asked what is the maximum estimated need in United States troops for an offensive against Germany. The answer was 15 to 17 divisions in 1942, or early 1943, including armored divisions. ADMIRAL TURNER then stated that 45 divisions was the maximum which could be transported and supplied by available shipping in sight.

ADMIRAL KING pointed out that the most mischievous naval operations which the Germans could make at this time would be a mass surface and submarine attack on convoy routes in the Atlantic. ADMIRAL STARK then stated that a most important target for the bombing operations against Germany should be shipyards where submarines and airplane carriers are being built. AIR CHIEF MARSHAL PORTAL agreed.

ADMIRAL POUND was given a copy of the American Naval building program. He stated to General Marshall that the United States Army should look into the matter of putting a force into North Africa if the British do, under either of the following conditions:

a. If invited by the French.

b. If Germany makes a move through the Iberian Peninsula.

In either case the attack should be a surprise.

22. BRITISH ESTIMATE OF ATTACK ON WEST COAST OF NORTH AMERICA. -

In response to a request from Admiral Stark, ADMIRAL POUND read to the Conference a note which had been prepared by the British Chiefs of Staff on the probable scale of attack on the West Coast of North America.

In view of the short time which the United States Chiefs of Staff had had to study the British Chiefs of Staff memorandum, further discussion on it was deferred. (See Annex 2)

U. S. SECRET
BRITISH MOST SECRET

      The meeting adjourned at 1:30 p.m., with instructions given that the Planning Committee would meet in the afternoon and that the Chiefs of Staff Conference would reconvene at 10:30 a.m., December 25th.

2 ENCLOSURES:
    Annex 1. - American-British Strategy WW-1.
    Annex 2. - Probable maximum scale of Enemy Attack on West Coast of
              North America.

U. S. SECRET
BRITISH MOST SECRET

ANNEX 1
To
ABC-4
JCCSs-1

TO BE KEPT UNDER LOCK AND KEY

W.W.-1.(U.S. Revised)

It is requested that special care may be taken to ensure the secrecy of this document.

WASHINGTON WAR CONFERENCE

AMERICAN-BRITISH STRATEGY.

MEMORANDUM BY THE BRITISH CHIEFS OF STAFF.
REVISED BY U.S. CHIEFS OF STAFF.

I. GRAND STRATEGY

1   At the A-B* Staff conversations in February, 1941, it was agreed that Germany was the predominant member of the Axis Powers, and consequently the Atlantic and European area was considered to be the decisive theatre

2. Much has happened since February last, but notwithstanding the entry of Japan into the War, our view remains that Germany is still the prime enemy and her defeat is the key to victory Once Germany is defeated, the collapse of Italy and the defeat of Japan must follow.

3. In our considered opinion, therefore, it should be a cardinal principle of A-B strategy that only the minimum of force necessary for the safeguarding of vital interests in other theatres should be diverted from operations against Germany

II ESSENTIAL FEATURES OF OUR STRATEGY

4. The essential features of the above grand strategy are as follows. Each will be examined in greater detail later in this paper.

    a. The realization of the victory programme of armaments, which first and foremost requires the security of the main areas of war industry.

Note:-
 * For brevity the abbreviated
   A-B is used to denote
   American-British

U. S. SECRET
BRITISH MOST SECRET

    b. The maintenance of essential communications.

    c. Closing and tightening the ring round Germany.

    d. Wearing down and undermining German resistance by air bombardment, blockade, subversive activities, and propaganda.

    e. The continuous development of offensive action against Germany.

    f. Maintaining only such positions in the Eastern theatre as will safeguard vital interests and deny to Japan access to raw materials vital to her continuous war effort while we are concentrating on the defeat of Germany.

   III. STEPS TO BE TAKEN IN 1942 TO PUT INTO EFFECT THE ABOVE

GENERAL POLICY.

THE SECURITY OF AREAS OF WAR PRODUCTION.

5. In so far as these are likely to be attacked, the main areas of war industry are situated in:-

    a. The United Kingdom.

    b. Continental United States, particularly the West Coast.

    c. Russia.

6. THE UNITED KINGDOM. To safeguard the United Kingdom it will be necessary to maintain at all times the minimum forces required to defeat invasion.

7. THE UNITED STATES. The main centres of production on or near the West Coast of United States must be protected from Japanese sea-borne attack. This will be facilitated by holding Hawaii and Alaska. We consider that a Japanese invasion of the United States on a large scale is highly improbable, whether Hawaii or Alaska is held or not.

8. The probable scale of attack and the general nature of the forces required for the defense of the United States are matters for the United States Chiefs of Staff to assess.

9. RUSSIA. It will be essential to afford the Russians material assistance to enable them to maintain their hold on Leningrad, Moscow and the oilfields of the Caucasus, and to continue their war effort.

U.S. SECRET
BRITISH MOST SECRET

MAINTENANCE OF COMMUNICATIONS.

10. The main sea routes which must be secured are:-

   a. From U.S.A. to the United Kingdom.

   b. From U.S.A. and the United Kingdom to North Russia.

   c. The various routes from the United Kingdom and U.S.A. to Freetown, South America and the Cape.

   d. The routes in the Indian Ocean to the Red Sea and Persian Gulf, to India and Burma, to the East Indies and to Australasia.

   e. The route through the Panama Canal, and U.S. coastal traffic.

   f. The Pacific routes from United States and the Panama Canal to Alaska, Hawaii, Australia and the Far East. In addition to the above routes, we shall do everything possible to open up and secure the Mediterranean route.

11. The main air routes which must be secured are:-

   a. From the U.S. to South America, Freetown, Takoradi, and Cairo.

   b. From Cairo to Karachi, Calcutta, China, Malaya, Philippines, Australasia.

   c. From the U.S. to Australia via Hawaii, Christmas Island, Canton, Palmyra, Samoa, Fiji, New Caledonia.

   d. The routes from Australia to the Philippines and Malaya via the Netherlands East Indies.

   e. From the U.S. to the U.K. via Newfoundland, Canada, Greenland and Iceland.

   f. From the U.S. to the U.K. via the Azores.

   g. From the U.S. to Vladivostok via Alaska.

12. The security of these routes involves:-

   a. Well-balanced A - B naval and air dispositions.

   b. Holding and capturing essential sea bases. The main sea bases which are, or may be, required, apart from the terminal points to the various routes, are:-

U.S. SECRET
BRITISH MOST SECRET

        Bermuda
        Iceland
        Gibraltar or the Canaries
        The Azores
        Cape Verdes
        Freetown
        Dakar
        Madagascar
        Ceylon
        Hawaii
        Samoa

    c. Holding and capturing essential air bases. The main air bases which are or may be required, apart from the terminal points to the various routes, are:-

Newfoundland	Basra
Greenland	Teheran
Iceland	Kuibyshev
Azores	Dakar
Bermuda	Karachi
Trinidad	Calcutta
Belem	Hawaii
Natal	Christmas Island
Freetown	Palmyra
Ascension Island	Canton
Takoradi	Samoa
Lagos	Fiji
Kano	New Caledonia
Ft. Lamy	Townsville
Khartoum	Darwin
Massaua	Glencurry
Cairo	Koepang (Timor)
Habbaniya	Soerabaja

CLOSING AND TIGHTENING THE RING AROUND GERMANY.

13.   This ring may be defined as a line running roughly as follows:

    ARCHANGEL - BLACK SEA - ANATOLIA - THE NORTHERN SEABOARD OF THE MEDITERRANEAN - THE WESTERN SEABOARD OF EUROPE.

    The main object will be to strengthen this ring, and close the gaps in it, by sustaining the Russian front, by arming and supporting Turkey, by increasing our strength in the Middle East, and by gaining possession of the whole North African coast.

U.S. SECRET
BRITISH MOST SECRET

14. If this ring can be closed, the blockade of Germany and Italy will be complete, and German eruptions, e.g. towards the Persian Gulf, or to the Atlantic seaboard of Africa, will be prevented. Furthermore, the seizing of the North African coast may open the Mediterranean to convoys, thus enormously shortening the route to the Middle East and saving considerable tonnage now employed in the long haul around the Cape.

THE UNDERMINING AND WEARING DOWN OF THE GERMAN RESISTANCE

15. In 1942, the main methods of wearing down Germany's resistance will be:-

    a. Ever-increasing air bombardment by British and American Forces

    b. Assistance to Russia's offensive by all available means.

    c. The blockade.

    d. The maintenance of the spirit of revolt in the occupied countries, and the organization of subversive movements.

DEVELOPMENT OF LAND OFFENSIVES ON THE CONTINENT

16. It does not seem likely that in 1942 any large scale land offensive against Germany, except on the Russian front, will be possible. We must, however, be ready to take advantage of any opening that may result from the wearing down process referred to in paragraph 15 to conduct limited land offensives.

17. In 1943 the way may be clear for a return to the Continent, via the Scandinavian Peninsula, across the Mediterranean, from Turkey into the Balkans, or by simultaneous landings in several of the occupied countries of Northwestern Europe. Such operations will be the prelude to the final assault on Germany itself, and the scope of the victory programme should be such as to provide means by which they can be carried out.

THE SAFEGUARDING OF VITAL INTERESTS IN THE EASTERN THEATRE

18. The security of Australia, New Zealand, and India must be maintained and Chinese resistance supported. Secondly, points of vantage from which an offensive against Japan can eventually be developed must be secured. Our immediate object must therefore be to hold:-

    a. Hawaii and Alaska.

    b. Singapore, the East Indies Barrier, and the Philippines.

U.S. SECRET
BRITISH MOST SECRET

       c.   Rangoon and the route to China.

       d.   The Maritime Provinces of Russia.

         The minimum forces required to hold the above will have to be a matter of mutual discussion.

U. S. SECRET
BRITISH MOST SECRET

ANNEX 2

PROBABLE MAXIMUM SCALE OF ENEMY ATTACK ON WEST COAST OF NORTH AMERICA

EXAMINATION OF PROBABLE FORM OF ENEMY ATTACK.

    1. Enemy attack on the western seaboard of North America might be undertaken with the object of reducing United States offensive power in the Pacific through material destruction at shipyards and bases and also with the object of containing forces in America.

    2. The following forms of attack have been considered: -

        a. Seaborne expeditions;

        b. Naval bombardment;

        c Carrier-borne air attacks;

        d. Mine-laying in ports and their approaches and attacks by human torpedoes.

SEABORNE EXPEDITIONS.

    3. So long as a United States capital ship force is retained in the Pacific, it is extremely improbable that the Japanese would venture to launch a large scale expedition against a North American objective without battleship cover. It must also be assumed that apart from the destroyer escorts for the convoys, destroyers would be essential for A/A and A/S protection for the battleships.

    4. The diagram attached* to this Annex illustrates the large distances to be covered and shows that even if the enemy secured Dutch Harbour and Hawaii, it would be necessary to carry out the refueling of destroyers at sea.

    While the refueling of an expedition at sea in hostile waters can not be ruled out positively, the complications and risks of such an operation on a large scale are sufficiently great to make it extremely unlikely. Added to this factor is the problem of maintaining a large scale expedition over 4,000 miles from its base.

* APPENDIX A

U. S. SECRET
BRITISH MOST SECRET

5. These difficulties do not apply so strongly to a small scale raiding force escorted by cruisers and aircraft carriers which have much greater endurance. For this reason it is necessary to take into account the possibility that a force comprising 10-15 fast merchant ships carrying up to 2 brigades on a low scale of transport might undertake a destructive raid.

NAVAL BOMBARDMENT.

6. For the reasons given above, the employment of enemy battleships any great distance to the eastward of Hawaii is improbable. Naval bombardment of important objectives on the west coast of North America is therefore likely to be restricted to bombardment by armoured ships other than ships of the line and cruisers.

CARRIER-BORNE AIR ATTACKS.

7. The employment of a carrier force escorted by cruisers for the air attack of important naval and industrial objectives is the most probable threat which has to be met. It is considered that the Japanese could make available a force of from 2-3 aircraft carriers escorted by 4 cruisers, without interfering with her dispositions for the other operations upon which she is now engaged. This would involve an attack by some 80-100 dive and/or torpedo bombers, with ship escort of approximately 24 fighters.

MINE-LAYING IN PORTS AND THEIR APPROACHES AND ATTACKS BY HUMAN TORPEDOES.

8. Mine-laying by raiders and submarines in coastal waters must be expected. The enemy's ability to carry out attacks by human torpedoes has, it is understood, been demonstrated at Hawaii. It cannot therefore be ignored.

CONCLUSIONS

So long as the United States maintains a battle fleet in the Pacific, large scale seaborne expeditions against the western seaboard of North America and the employment of capital ship forces in this area are considered impracticable. The most probable enemy threat is carrier-borne air attacks and sporadic naval bombardment, but a small scale destructive raid cannot be ignored. In view of the great distances over which these operations would have to be undertaken, it is probably not necessary to provide a strong scale of defense except at selected points of great importance, which can be covered by the normal form of coast and air defense supplemented by mobile land and air striking forces.

U. S. SECRET
BRITISH MOST SECRET

APPENDIX A TO
ANNEX 2

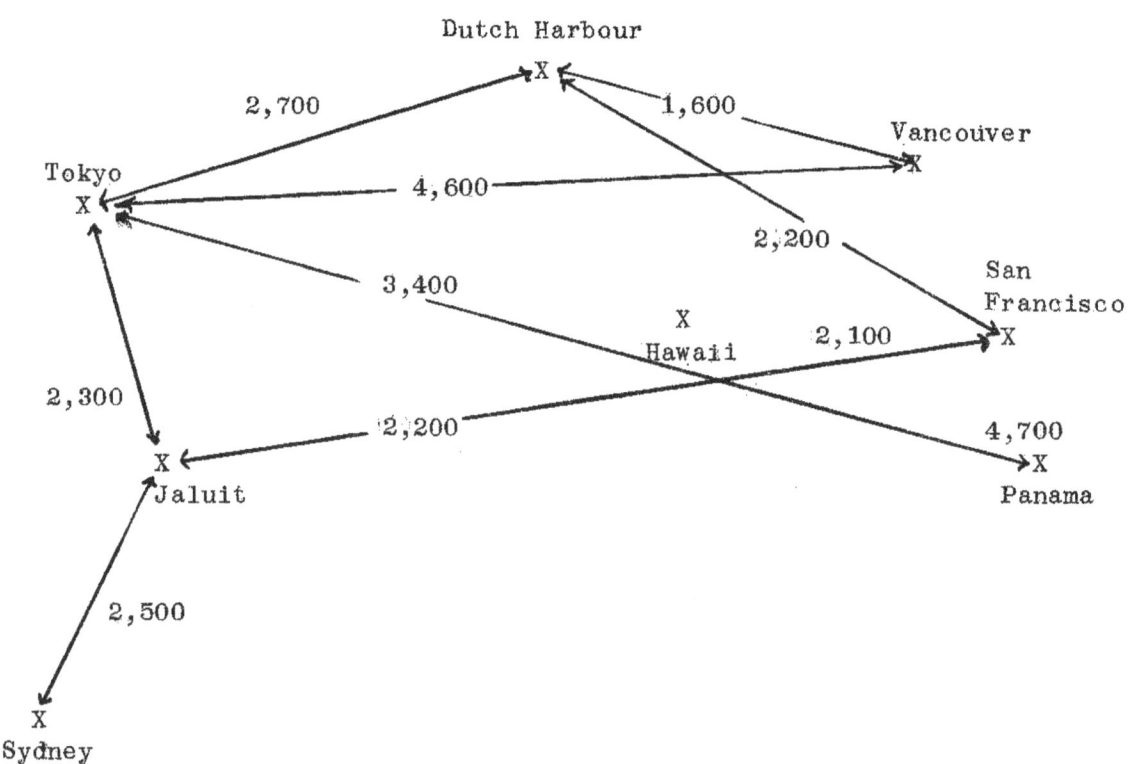

- 3 -

U. S. SECRET
BRITISH MOST SECRET

ABC 4
JCCSs-2   December 25, 1941

THE CHIEFS OF STAFF CONFERENCE

FEDERAL RESERVE BUILDING

WASHINGTON, D. C.

4 P. M., DECEMBER 25, 1941

Present

British Officers

    Admiral of the Fleet, Sir Dudley Pound, First Sea Lord and Chief of Naval Staff
    Field Marshal Sir John Dill
    Air Chief Marshal Sir Charles Portal, Chief of Air Staff

U. S. Naval Officers

    Admiral H. R. Stark, Chief of Naval Operations
    Admiral E. J. King, Commander-in-Chief, U. S. Fleet
    Rear Admiral F. J. Horne, Assistant Chief, Naval Operations
    Rear Admiral J. H. Towers, Chief, Bureau of Aeronautics
    Rear Admiral R. K. Turner, Director, War Plans Division

U. S. Army Officers

    General George C. Marshall, Commanding General of the Field Forces and Chief of Staff, U. S. Army
    Lieut. General H. H. Arnold, Chief of Army Air Forces and Deputy Chief of Staff, U. S. Army
    Brig. General D. D. Eisenhower, War Plans Division, W.D.G.S.

Joint Secretaries

    Colonel E. I. C. Jacob
    Captain J. L. McCrea, Aide to the Chief of Naval Operations
    Lieut. Col. P. M. Robinett, G-2, General Headquarters, U.S.A.
    Major W. T. Sexton, Asst. Secretary, General Staff, W.D.G.S.

1. PROGRAM OF PLANNING.-

    REAR ADMIRAL TURNER said that the Planning Committee had been working on two projects which were nearly completed:-

U. S. SECRET
BRITISH MOST SECRET

        a.   Outline plan proposed for peaceful occupation of North Africa.

        b.   Program of priorities in the Atlantic.

It was anticipated that they would be ready for presentation shortly.

2.   DISPOSITION OF THE MOUNT VERNON.-

GENERAL MARSHALL said that he had been given to understand that it was desired to alter the destination of the MOUNT VERNON.

ADMIRAL STARK stated that orders had been issued for the MOUNT VERNON to proceed to Singapore or any other place the British Admiralty desired, but stated that these instructions did not involve escort being furnished for the MOUNT VERNON by the United States. ADMIRAL POUND indicated that the British had no intention of asking the United States to furnish escort, and stated that he regarded such escort as being a responsibility of the Royal Navy.

3.   DIVERSION OF REINFORCEMENTS.-

GENERAL MARSHALL discussed the possible diversion of reinforcements to the Philippines. He stated that up to the present moment, he had had no opportunity to consult with Admiral Stark on the matter, but he had been called on to submit a list of troop and equipment departures and anticipation of arrivals in Australia. He read this data, a copy of which was furnished to the British Chiefs of Staff, (See Annex 1). He also stated that General Brett had been ordered to proceed immediately to Australia and place himself under the direction of General MacArthur, and to forward his recommendations as to the situation in the Philippine Islands. He stated that the question of his (General Brett's) continued subordination to General MacArthur would be determined later.

AIR CHIEF MARSHAL PORTAL mentioned that the Australian representatives in Washington had stated that unless ten million gallons of 100-octane gasoline could be forwarded to Australia immediately, the planes there would shortly be immobilized. GENERAL ARNOLD said that this is no problem so long as we can keep contact with Sumatra, as Sumatra furnishes this gasoline. AIR CHIEF MARSHAL PORTAL said that it was his understanding that the Sumatra gasoline was not satisfactory and that American-produced gasoline was involved.

GENERAL ARNOLD said that the only difficulty involved in the Sumatra gasoline was the aromatics in it, which affected adversely the self-sealing tanks. This difficulty had been anticipated and extra tanks for replacements were being forwarded to Australia. The new tanks would not be so affected by aromatics.

U. S. SECRET
BRITISH MOST SECRET

With reference to the diversion of reinforcements intended for the Philippine Islands, GENERAL MARSHALL said, "We do not have enough information at this time from General MacArthur to make a decision on this matter. However, we must not stand idle while waiting to know what he proposes. Until we know what the local situation is, we can not cut off reinforcements from him. We will know in 24 hours whether or not it is a fast withdrawal and where it goes, and whether or not pursuit planes can get to him."

AIR MARSHAL PORTAL asked if General MacArthur has any instructions relative to the disposal of airplanes if he can not operate in the Philippine Islands. GENERAL ARNOLD replied that the bombers are already operating from Australia. He further stated that it must be assumed that the man on the ground will do the right thing. He said that General MacArthur has a good air officer who can be counted on to dispose properly of the remaining pursuit planes.

AIR MARSHAL PORTAL asked if General MacArthur would send his pursuit to Singapore. He added further that it was difficult for any man on the spot to make a decision relative to the disposal of his own means; that the decision should be made here by the responsible group.

4. UNIFIED COMMAND.-

GENERAL MARSHALL then brought up the question of command. He said, "I express these as my personal views and not those as a result of consultation with the Navy or with my own War Plans Division. As a result of what I saw in France and from following our own experience, I feel very strongly that the most important consideration is the question of unity of command. The matters being settled here are mere details which will continuously reoccur unless settled in a broader way. With differences between groups and between services, the situation is impossible unless we operate on a frank and direct basis. I am convinced that there must be one man in command of the entire theater -- air, ground, and ships. We can not manage by cooperation. Human frailties are such that there would be emphatic unwillingness to place portions of troops under another service. If we make a plan for unified command now, it will solve nine-tenths of our troubles.

"There are difficulties in arriving at a single command, but they are much less than the hazards that must be faced if we do not achieve this. We never think alike -- there are the opinions of those on this side of the table and of the people on the other side; but as for myself, I am willing to go the limit to accomplish this. We must decide on a line of action here and not expect it to be done out there. I favor one man being in control, but operating under a controlled directive from here. We had to come to this in the first World War, but it was not until 1918 that it was accomplished and much valuable time, blood, and treasure had been needlessly sacrificed. If we could decide on a unified command now, it would be a great advance over what was accomplished during the World War."

U. S. SECRET
BRITISH MOST SECRET

AIR MARSHAL PORTAL said that the experience in London has been that the highest authority is the only one that can decide as to the allocation of forces; and when the allocation is decided upon, the directive has been formulated, and the forces allotted, everything else moves smoothly. If allocations are controlled from Washington, there should be no difficulty.

GENERAL MARSHALL said that the British and Americans are in complete agreement as to allocations; what he was speaking of was operations in the field.

5. DISPOSITION OF FORCES DESTINED FOR THE FAR EAST.-

AIR MARSHAL PORTAL said that the disposition of our forces must be planned first. This can be considered a Staff study, without commitments, based on ultimate dispositions under the following two conditions:

    a.   The Philippine Islands holding.

    b.   In case the Philippine Islands can not hold.

ADMIRAL KING said that he felt this study should probably have first priority.

ADMIRAL POUND inquired as to whether or not a study could be made of this entire problem, stating that it was of such an urgent nature that other things should be set aside, and inquired as to the proper directive. The consensus was that this should be done, and the senior members of the Planning Committee were called in and so informed.

ADMIRAL STARK requested Rear Admiral Turner to give his opinion as to the question of allocations of aircraft reinforcements now going to the Far East. REAR ADMIRAL TURNER replied that responsibility should be given to General MacArthur if he is in a position to accept it where the planes are to be delivered; otherwise to General Brett.

There followed a discussion as to the proper directive, and several preliminary directives were drafted by various members of the Chiefs of Staff group.

As the American officers were due at the White House for a meeting, the conference adjourned at 5:20 p.m.

After the main conference adjourned, ADMIRAL POUND called into consultation Colonel Jacob, Commander Coleridge, and Colonel Robinett, and discussed the various phases of proposed directives. A directive for submission to the senior members of the Planning Committee was drawn up and submitted to

U. S. SECRET
BRITISH MOST SECRET

Rear Admiral Turner, who at the time was presiding at another meeting in the Federal Reserve Building. It was understood that Rear Admiral Turner and Brigadier General Gerow were not to accept the directive unless it was entirely agreeable to them, and Brigadier General Gerow was so informed by Colonel Robinett.

1 ENCLOSURE:

    Annex 1 - Utilization of U. S. Forces
             in Australia.

U. S. SECRET
BRITISH MOST SECRET

ANNEX 1

MEMORANDUM FOR THE PRESIDENT:

Subject: Utilization of U. S. Forces in Australia.

1. U. S. combat troops now in Australia and expected there at approximate dates indicated:

    a. Now present:

        18 pursuit planes
        52 dive bombers
        Elements of 2 regiments of 75 mm. artillery, (28 of its 48 guns are present. The 20 others are on a slow boat which left Samoa December 18). Only 500 rounds of 75 mm. ammunition available until about January 8, when 5,000 rounds will arrive at Brisbane.

    b. Expected soon:

      (1) 55 pursuit planes and crews (about January 8).

      (2) To begin arriving in theater on or about January 3; three heavy bombers per day until a total of eighty is assembled. These planes are now directed to report to General MacArthur for orders upon arrival at Bangalore. For operations of the immediate future, there is an adequate number of 500 lb. and smaller bombs, as well as 56 - 1000 lb. bombs on the convoy now proceeding from Brisbane to Port Darwin. Already at Darwin are 560 of the 500 lb. type, with 260 at Port Moresby.

      (3) 55 pursuit and crews, about January 16.

      (4) 70 pursuit planes and crews, about January 18. (It is possible that capacity of ship will be found to be 40 planes).

      (5) A pursuit group, complete as to materiel, including 80 planes, will leave San Diego on the KITTY HAWK about January 10. Additional ships will be necessary for the personnel.

U. S. SECRET
BRITISH MOST SECRET

NOTE: Dates at which there can arrive in Australia necessary ground crews and maintenance facilities for all the planes listed in the first three shipments are still uncertain. But, including the pilots sent from the Philippine Islands to Australia, and with maximum help from Australian sources, all planes can temporarily operate usefully, pending the arrival of necessary maintenance units. Including planes already arrived or en route, the U. S. Air Corps has already allocated a grand total of 333 pursuit planes for shipment to Australia. The above represents the maximum capacity of ships now available.

2. All U. S. forces in Australia are to be commanded by Major General George H. Brett. General Brett has been under orders to take his instructions from General MacArthur. However, the situation in the Philippines apparently has changed to an extent that makes it improbable that pursuit plane reinforcements can be forwarded to General MacArthur. Therefore, the following instructions were sent General Brett at Chungking December 24th A.M.:

PROCEED AS QUICKLY AS POSSIBLE TO AUSTRALIA TO ASSUME COMMAND OF U. S. ARMY INTERESTS IN THAT REGION. REPORT ARRIVAL AND FOLLOW IMMEDIATELY WITH A PRELIMINARY RECOMMENDATION OF ACTION TO BE TAKEN IN VIEW OF SITUATION IN PHILIPPINES AT THAT TIME. MARSHALL.

3. It is intended that General Brett's status with regard to subordination to General MacArthur will be settled in the light of the situation in the Philippines at the time of his arrival in Australia.

4. The United States and British Chiefs of Staff jointly recommend:

a. That immediate request be made upon Australian, British, and Dutch authorities to render maximum assistance to the U. S. Commander in Australia in the preparation of his air elements for combat, and in the establishment and protection of the necessary bases, with a view to the immediate entry of these air forces into action.

b. That the responsible British and American Commanders be directed to make preliminary arrangements for effective combat cooperation between other forces of the Associated Powers and the U. S. Air Force in the Southwestern Pacific. Preliminary plans for early support of Singapore to be initiated at once.

5. The current U. S. Air Corps objective in the Southwestern Pacific, exclusive of China and Russia, is:

            2 Heavy Groups   -- 80 planes
            2 Medium Groups   --114 planes
            6 Pursuit Groups --480 planes
            Necessary base and auxiliary units.

This strength can be attained as rapidly as shipping facilities permit.

U. S. SECRET
BRITISH MOST SECRET

ABC-4
JCCSs-3
December 26, 1941

THE CHIEFS OF STAFF CONFERENCE

FEDERAL RESERVE BUILDING

WASHINGTON, D. C.

3 P.M., DECEMBER 26, 1941

Present

British Officers

    Admiral of the Fleet, Sir Dudley Pound, First Sea Lord and Chief of Naval Staff
    Field Marshal Sir John Dill
    Air Chief Marshal Sir Charles Portal, Chief of Air Staff
    Admiral Sir Charles Little, Joint Staff Mission
    Lieut. General Sir Colville Wemyss, Joint Staff Mission
    Air Marshal A. T. Harris, Joint Staff Mission

U. S. Naval Officers

    Admiral H. R. Stark, Chief of Naval Operations
    Admiral E. J. King, Commander-in-Chief, U. S. Fleet
    Rear Admiral W. R. Sexton, President, General Board
    Rear Admiral F. J. Horne, Assistant Chief of Naval Operations
    Rear Admiral J. H. Towers, Chief, Bureau of Aeronautics
    Rear Admiral R. K. Turner, Director, War Plans Division
    Major General Thomas Holcomb, Commandant, U. S. Marine Corps

U. S. Army Officers

    General George C. Marshall, Commanding General of the Field Forces and Chief of Staff, U. S. Army
    Lieut. General H. H. Arnold, Chief of Army Air Forces and Deputy Chief of Staff, U. S. Army
    Brigadier General L. T. Gerow, Chief of War Plans Division

U. S. SECRET
BRITISH MOST SECRET

Joint Secretaries

    Brigadier L. C. Hollis, R. M.
    Colonel E. I. C. Jacob
    Commander R. D. Coleridge, R. N.
    Captain J. L. McCrea, Aide to Chief of Naval Operations
    Lieut. Colonel Paul McD. Robinett, G-2, GHQ
    Major W. T. Sexton, G. S. C., Assistant Secretary W.D.G.S.

1. PRIORITIES FOR U.S. AND U.K. OVERSEAS EXPEDITIONS IN THE ATLANTIC OCEAN - (ABC-4/1)

ADMIRAL STARK read the proposed plan and there followed a general discussion.

ADMIRAL TURNER said that the Joint Planning Committee recognized the importance of the North African project (operation GYMNAST), but were not at this stage prepared to make recommendations on the relative priority of this and the other projects mentioned in paragraph 1(b) of their Report. The limitations on shipping and naval escort forces made it impossible to carry out the North African plan, and simultaneously relieve the British forces in Ireland and Iceland. If the North African project were carried out as envisaged, each power would produce the requisite amount of shipping for its own forces, but would have none extra available to lend to the other power. In addition, shipping required for the British part of "GYMNAST" would seriously interfere with British reinforcements to the Middle East.

The British delegation considered two possible moments at which the North African project would have to be put into effect as rapidly as possible; either (a) when British forces, moving from the eastward, had occupied Tripoli, or (b) when Marshal Petain resigned, as had been thought possible. The second occasion now seemed unlikely to occur, though the first remained; and it was felt that the Chiefs of Staff should obtain a decision from the President and the Prime Minister as to whether or not it had been decided to make a political approach to the French authorities in order to obtain an invitation to enter French North Africa. The British forces for "GYMNAST" were ready but their removal from the United Kingdom would leave the defense of the British Isles weak unless the United States took over the Iceland and Ireland Commitments. Nevertheless, the British view was that the North African project would have to go forward if an invitation were received.

It was generally agreed that, for the purposes of paragraph 3 of the Joint Planning Committee's Report, the major operations in the Atlantic area, only one of which could be carried out at one time, could be stated to be:-

U. S. SECRET
BRITISH MOST SECRET

        Northwest Africa.
        West Africa.
        Northeast Brazil and the Cape Verde Islands.
        Northern Ireland and Iceland.

The occupation of the Canaries (by invitation), the Azores, and of Aruba and Curacao, fell into the category of minor operations. Further consideration would have to be given to the status of the Madagascar operation.

It appeared that the British Chiefs of Staff understood that this report (see Annex 1), was accepted. However, the understanding of the United States Chiefs of Staff was that it was accepted in principle but should be restudied and resubmitted for further consideration.

2. NORTHWEST AFRICA PROJECT

The British delegation was of the opinion that it would take German forces six weeks to prepare to invade Spain, and, without Spanish cooperation, a further six weeks to become firmly established in the South of Spain. It was pointed out that this estimate was based on the best information available to the British, and took account of the fact that the Germans at the present time had no forces readily available to undertake the operation. It was realized that with Spanish help the date of arrival in South Spain could be considerably accelerated.

ADMIRAL TURNER explained that the Joint Planning Committee felt that only Casablanca should be used, in the first instance, as the minor ports were difficult to protect from submarine attack and effective anti-air protection could only be given to one port. He pointed out that the size of the North African expedition as envisaged by the Joint Planning Committee was greatly in excess of anything previously considered, and the implications on shipping were therefore enormous. Was this increase in size essential - particularly with regard to air? The British view was that the German Air Force was already stretched almost to its limit. It was decided that consideration of the size of the forces required should be deferred.

It was also pointed out that one reason why large forces had to be envisaged was that the French authorities would in all probability only issue the invitation if the bait were, in their opinion, adequate. It was suggested that the French air force in North Africa might, in the early stages, prove of some value in spite of its known lack of spares, but GENERAL ARNOLD said that from a recent conversation he had had with a French officer who had recently left North Africa, he understood that only 40 of the French aircraft were capable of taking the air.

U. S. SECRET
BRITISH MOST SECRET

       The U. S.-British Chiefs of Staff gave general approval to the Report, Annex 2, subject to certain amendments, and subject to further consideration of the strength of the forces required for the expedition.

2 Enclosures:
    Annex 1 – Priorities for United States and United Kingdom Overseas
              Expedition in Atlantic Ocean – ABC-4/1; W.W.(J.P.C.)1
    Annex 2 – Northwest Africa Project (Super-GYMNAST) – ABC-4/2; W.W.
           (J.P.C.)2

U. S. SECRET
BRITISH MOST SECRET

ANNEX 1

This paper was not approved but was returned to the Joint Planning Committee for reconsideration and re-submission for further consideration.

U. S. SERIAL ABC-4/1
BRITISH SERIAL W.W.(JPC) 1

PRIORITIES FOR UNITED STATES AND UNITED KINGDOM OVERSEAS EXPEDITIONS IN THE ATLANTIC OCEAN

REPORT BY THE U.S.-BRITISH JOINT PLANNING COMMITTEE

1. One of the directives to the Joint Planning Committee issued by the Chiefs of Staff Committee on December 24, 1941, may be summarized as follows:

   Study and report outline plans for the overseas employment of United States and British troops in the Atlantic region, indicating recommended relative priorities of importance:

   a   The relief by United States troops of British troops in Iceland and North Ireland.

   b   The occupation by invitation of the following positions:

   (1) The Azores.
   (2) The Cape Verde Islands.
   (3) The Canary Islands.
   (4) French West Africa.
   (5) French North Africa
   (6) Diego Suarez in Madagascar.
   (7) Curacao and Aruba.
   (8) Northeast Brazil.

2. The Joint Planning Committee recommends that the initial occupation by invitation of the foreign positions indicated in the directive should be allocated as follows:

   a   To the United States - the occupation of the Cape Verde Islands, French West Africa, Curacao and Aruba, Northeast Brazil.

U. S. SECRET
BRITISH MOST SECRET

   <u>b</u> To the United Kingdom - the occupation of the
     Azores, the Canary Islands, and Diego Suarez
     in Madagascar.

   <u>c</u> To the United States and the United Kingdom acting
     jointly - the occupation of French North Africa.

 3. If the operation in French North Africa as submitted in our plan (U.S. Serial ABC-4/2, British Serial W.W.(J.P.C.)2) is undertaken, we see no prospect of any major movements being carried out in the Atlantic area for at least three months, and normal reinforcements to the eastward from the United Kingdom will be severely curtailed.

 4. No major overseas operations can be performed by the United States unless adequate shipping is immediately made available for preparation as troop transports.

Washington, D. C.

 25th December, 1941.

U. S. SECRET
BRITISH MOST SECRET

ANNEX 2

This paper was not approved but was returned to the Joint Planning Committee for reconsideration and resubmission for further consideration.

U. S. SERIAL ABC-4/2
BRITISH SERIAL W.W.(J.P.C.)2

PROJECT - GYMNAST

We submit below a provisional examination of the project for joint operations in Northwest Africa. Our examination is based on the following hypotheses:-

    a That we receive an actual invitation or reasonable assurance there will be only token resistance.

    b That owing to their pre-occupations on the Eastern front, it would take the Germans six weeks to prepare to invade Spain, the forces now in France being unsuitable, and that without Spanish cooperation it would take them about a further six weeks to become firmly established with land and air forces in the South of Spain after they had crossed the Pyrenees. We therefore anticipate a period of about three months before a heavy scale of attack could be mounted against French North Africa from Spain. Spain would probably offer no very effective resistance on the mainland to a German invasion, but would not give the Germans free entry and full facilities. Once the mainland had been invaded our forces would probably be admitted freely into Spanish Morocco.

    c That the Germans are not established in French North Africa in sufficient strength to oppose effectively the occupation of French Morocco.

OBJECTIVE.

We consider our primary object is to establish ourselves in Northern French Morocco as quickly as possible. This would provide a base from which Spanish Morocco could be occupied at short notice and thus block Germany's line of advance from Spain. The area would also form a base from which Allied control of all North Africa could be extended.

U. S. SECRET
BRITISH MOST SECRET

BASE.

The only suitable main base in the area is Casablanca. This port is well developed, served by railways and roads, and lies outside the Straits of Gibraltar. It would be unsound to use as a main base any port inside the Straits as the sea communications to it from the Atlantic would be liable to interruption once the Germans reached South Spain. Initially, owing to scarcity of anti-aircraft defenses and air forces, a single main base must be used for the whole force in North Africa.

ESTABLISHMENT OF BASE.

There is the possibility of at least token resistance by French forces at Casablanca, which has a considerable garrison and coast defenses. The first force to enter must, therefore, be combat loaded. The United States Marine Division is eminently suitable for this task, and there would be much greater likelihood of French acquiescence in the entry of American forces rather than British.

SUPPORT TO FRENCH IN TUNISIA.

The immediate result of our forces gaining an entry in Western Morocco, or perhaps a condition of their entry, would be a demand from the French for support against a German threat in Tunisia. We must, therefore, have a suitable force prepared to meet this. This might consist of an Armored Brigade, an Infantry Brigade, two Anti-aircraft Regiments, and three Fighter Squadrons. The forces should be ready to go straight through by sea to, say, Algiers almost simultaneously with the arrival of the advance guard at Casablanca.

DEFENSE OF MOROCCAN AREA.

It will be essential to get sufficient forces into the Casablanca area in the early stages to avoid the possibility of the expedition being driven out by German air forces operating from Southern Spain. This points to the very early establishment of adequate air forces and anti-aircraft defenses.

The early arrival of a substantial Army contingent is also essential in order to rally the French and Spanish forces and secure the key positions in Morocco.

The joint forces which we should aim at landing during the first three months are estimated at:-

U. S. SECRET
BRITISH MOST SECRET

      1 Marine (combat loaded) Amphibious Division
      3 Infantry Divisions
      2 Armored Divisions
  320 First line fighter aircraft
   57 First line medium bomber aircraft
   57 First line light bomber aircraft
   63 First line observation aircraft
  120 Heavy anti-aircraft guns
  216 Light anti-aircraft guns
      Base and L. of C. units

As further forces become available, all points of entry along the coast will be secured.

TOTAL FORCES REQUIRED.

The total forces ULTIMATELY required to hold French North Africa against possible German attacks through Spain and Italy, and to open the Mediterranean route by providing air cover along the coast, will depend on the assistance that may be furnished by the French and Spanish. The combined British and United States forces might amount to about:

    2½ - 2 Armored Divisions
    5 - 3 Infantry Divisions
        Anti-aircraft weapons (350 heavy and 700 light)
    First line aircraft:
      800 Pursuit
      105 Heavy Bombardment
      228 Medium Bombardment
      171 Light Bombardment
      100 Naval Patrol

JOINT AMERICAN-BRITISH EFFORT NECESSARY.

Neither country has sufficient forces available to undertake the whole commitment single-handed in a short time. It must, therefore, be a joint expedition. At present the area is one of British strategic responsibility, as defined in ABC-1. As soon as decision is reached on the operation, it will be necessary to determine responsibility for command so that detailed planning can proceed.

U.S. SECRET
BRITISH MOST SECRET

NAVAL FORCES

BRITISH.

Unless there is reason to believe that enemy surface units are loose in the Atlantic, close protection of British convoys by heavy ships or aircraft carriers will not be essential. Protection provided by the Home Fleet watching the northern passages and by Force H in the Gibraltar area should be sufficient.

There will probably be 6 British convoys, each divided into a fast and slow portion, sailing from the United Kingdom at about fortnightly intervals. This amounts to doubling the rate of sailing of normal United Kingdom to Cape convoys and the extra escorts will have to be withdrawn from trade protection for a considerable period.

UNITED STATES.

The U. S. Atlantic Fleet will provide appropriate protection and support for the transit and landing of U. S. Expeditionary Forces.

AMERICAN CONVOY ESCORTS.

        a   Advance American Division -
              One Marine Division embarked in 15 vessels escorted by units from Task Force Three.

        b   Remainder of initial U. S. forces -
              Three convoys at about one month intervals, escorted by units withdrawn from Task Forces Three and Four. Successive logistic convoys require escorts withdrawn from Task Force Four.

TIMINGS.

    D-1 is the day on which the order is given to mount the expedition.

        a   U. S. FORCES
              The U. S. Marine Division could reach Casablanca on D-20.

        b   BRITISH FORCES
              The first British convoy could reach Algiers on D____, or Casablanca on D____. Subsequently the despatch of the remaining British forces, totalling 1 armored and 2 infantry divisions with ancillary troops would take about another____ weeks. Its movement would therefore be complete about D____.

U. S. SECRET
BRITISH MOST SECRET

SUMMARY OF PLAN.

    <u>a</u> U. S. Marine Division, combat loaded and closely supported by United States Naval forces, to secure an entry into Casablanca, against sporadic opposition if necessary.

    <u>b</u> A British force consisting of:-
        1 Armored Brigade,
        1 Infantry Brigade Group,
        2 Anti-aircraft Regiments,
        3 Fighter Squadrons,

to be ready to move in practically simultaneously with <u>a</u> to Tunisia in case the French demand support in that area; otherwise into Casablanca in support of the advance guard.

    <u>c</u> Main body to follow <u>a</u> and <u>b</u>:-
        1 American Army Division.
        1 American Armored Division.
        2 British Divisions.
        1 British Armored Division (less detachments in <u>b</u>).

        Air Forces:
          320 First line fighter aircraft
           57 First line medium bomber aircraft
           57 First line light bomber aircraft
           63 First line observation aircraft.

    <u>d</u> Base and L. of C. organizations. Air defenses of the base area to be found by the British initially.

    Each country to provide its own domestic base administrative services, sharing the base area and port facilities.

    U. S. to provide as high a proportion of engineer, technical, stevedore, and labor units for development of static base installations, aerodromes, etc.

The ultimate force to be built up as rapidly as possible.

U. S. SECRET
BRITISH MOST SECRET

ABC-4
JCCSs-4

THE CHIEFS OF STAFF CONFERENCE

FEDERAL RESERVE BUILDING

WASHINGTON, D. C.

3 P.M., DECEMBER 27, 1941.

Present

British Officers

    Admiral of the Fleet, Sir Dudley Pound, First Sea Lord and Chief of Naval Staff
    Field Marshal Sir John Dill
    Air Chief Marshal Sir Charles Portal, Chief of Air Staff
    Admiral Sir Charles Little, Joint Staff Mission
    Lieut. General Sir Colville Wemyss, Joint Staff Mission
    Air Marshal A. T. Harris, Joint Staff Mission
    Brigadier V. Dykes, Director of Plans, War Office
    Air Commodore W. F. Dickson, Director of Plans, Air Ministry
    Captain C. E. Lambe, R.N., Deputy Director of Plans, Admiralty

U. S. Naval Officers

    Admiral H. R. Stark, Chief of Naval Operations
    Admiral E. J. King, Commander-in-Chief, U. S. Fleet
    Rear Admiral W. R. Sexton, President, General Board
    Rear Admiral F. J. Horne, Assistant Chief, Naval Operations
    Rear Admiral J. H. Towers, Chief, Bureau of Aeronautics
    Rear Admiral R. K. Turner, Director, War Plans Division
    Major General Thomas Holcomb, Commandant, U. S. Marine Corps

U. S. Army Officers

    General George C. Marshall, Commanding General of the Field Forces and Chief of Staff.
    Lieut. General H. H. Arnold, Chief of Army Air Forces and Deputy Chief of Staff
    Brigadier General L. T. Gerow, Chief of War Plans Division.

U. S. SECRET
BRITISH MOST SECRET

Joint Secretaries

> Brigadier L. C. Hollis, R. M.
> Colonel E. I. C. Jacob
> Commander R. D. Coleridge, R. N.
> Captain J. L. McCrea, Aide to Chief of Naval Operations
> Lt. Colonel P. M. Robinett, G-2, GHQ, U. S. Army
> Major W. T. Sexton, Assistant Secretary, W.D.G.S.

1. ABC 4/1 -- PRIORITIES FOR UNITED STATES - UNITED KINGDOM EXPEDITIONS IN THE ATLANTIC OCEAN.-

ADMIRAL STARK presented a revised draft of ABC 4/1 to the Conference.

ADMIRAL POUND said that he understood the Report of the Joint Planning Committee had already been approved, and that he could not understand why a new draft was being submitted.

REAR ADMIRAL TURNER explained the changes. He said that copies of the changes had been furnished the British Section, but that apparently they had not been able to see them before the meeting.

ADMIRAL STARK said that there were few changes. The greater part of the paper had been previously agreed to.

After some further discussion, it was agreed that the paper should be referred to the Joint Planning Committee for reconsideration by both sections and then resubmitted to the Chiefs of Staff at the next meeting.

2. ABC 4/2 -- PLAN FOR EXPEDITION TO NORTHWEST AFRICA.-

ADMIRAL STARK brought up ABC 4/2, copies of which were distributed.

AIR MARSHAL PORTAL said that, with reference to the airplane allocations under this operation, he was horrified at the large number of planes contemplated; he thought it would be a mistake to send such a large number of planes to a theater of operations where they might not be utilized. He pointed out that in allocating planes, the large strategy must be the primary consideration, rather than local requirements; that in the matter of Greece it was realized that there was an insufficient number of troops and planes, yet those available were allocated despite the expectation that this force would be knocked down. Although this happened, the strategic importance of this operation was great because it delayed the attack on Russia for two months. He urged that in making allocations, the figures be viewed in the spirit of economy, that is, the minimum number that it would be safe to have.

U. S. SECRET
BRITISH MOST SECRET

GENERAL ARNOLD said that he had also objected to the large number of planes allocated, and thought the paper should be again referred to the Joint Planning Committee for further consideration.

GENERAL MARSHALL agreed that the paper should be referred back to the Planning Committee. He pointed out, however, that this operation might result in the first contact between American and German troops. Success should not be jeopardized by failure to provide adequate means. A failure in this first venture would have an extremely adverse effect on the morale of the American people. In summing up, he said that this first operation, although in some respects a minor one, could not be treated in a routine manner.

It was agreed that the paper would be referred back to the Joint Planning Committee for reconsideration, in the light of the discussion which had taken place, and revised draft submitted to the Chiefs of Staff at the next meeting.

3. AMERICAN - BRITISH STRATEGY.-

ADMIRAL STARK brought up WW/1, Joint American - British Strategy, which had been discussed previously.

REAR ADMIRAL TURNER said that the original British memorandum had not been fully agreed to.

ADMIRAL POUND said that the papers had been agreed to as the basis for our joint strategy, subject to some amendments which had been agreed to and to the inclusion of a revised paragraph on air routes as proposed by General Arnold.

ADMIRAL STARK agreed with Admiral Pound.

It was agreed that the paper would be referred back to the Joint Planning Committee and a revised draft incorporating the agreed amendments and the revised paragraph on routes should be submitted to the Chiefs of Staff at the next meeting.

4. PROGRAM OF WORK OF THE JOINT PLANNING COMMITTEE.-

REAR ADMIRAL TURNER listed the various papers now in the hands of the Joint Planning Committee as follows:

    a. WW/1 -- Grand Strategy.

    b. ABC-4/2 -- Expedition to Northwest Africa.

    c. Diversion of Reinforcements in the Far East.

U. S. SECRET
BRITISH MOST SECRET

It was suggested that a definite statement of priorities should be presented to the Chiefs of Staff at the next meeting. In the meantime, the Joint Planning Committee was to concentrate on the directive concerning the disposal of reinforcements en route to the Far East.

5. UNITY OF COMMAND.-

ADMIRAL STARK asked Admiral Pound if he cared to discuss the matter of unity of command for the Far East as proposed by General Marshall.

ADMIRAL POUND stated that he would like to get it clear in his mind what the United States means by unity of command, particularly how Naval matters would be dealt with.

GENERAL MARSHALL said that it would be impossible to choose anyone for supreme command who would have full technical knowledge of all services. He felt, however, that the matter of appointing a supreme commander would be bound up in the assumption that a man of good judgment would be selected; otherwise the whole project would be a failure. He felt that a man with good judgment and unity of command has a distinct advantage over a man with brilliant judgment who must rely on cooperation.

The whole matter, he said, rests on the consideration as to whether a directive could be drawn which would leave the Supreme Commander with enough power to improve the situation and still not give him power to destroy national interests or to exploit one theater without due consideration to another.

He then read a suggested form of letter, (See Annex 1,) copies of which were distributed, of instructions to the Supreme Commander, which he stated was purely a form and a basis for further discussion concerning the Far Eastern area. Similar directives might be possible for other areas.

In urging the adoption of unity of command in the Far East, GENERAL MARSHALL said that the Associated Powers are opposed in that area by an enemy who has unity of command in its highest sense; that in light of the present conditions out there, any action whatsoever along this line would be an improvement. The situation in this respect could not be made worse than it exists at present.

ADMIRAL POUND asked, on the assumption that four countries were involved, and a Supreme Commander were chosen for instance, from Power X, who would be on his Staff?

GENERAL MARSHALL replied that, personally, he envisaged a small staff, one representative from each Government possibly, who would act as a sort of liaison officer with local forces. The commander would possess two mobile elements -- one, sea-going vessels and the other, bombardment aviation.

U. S. SECRET
BRITISH MOST SECRET

He said that at the present time the situation in the Far East is tragic; that General Brereton, who was the air officer in the Philippines, had left the Philippines with heavy bombers and had been able to establish some contact with local commanders in Borneo and had ended up in Surabaya, Java. The information from General Brereton has been the most heartening from the Far East in the past few days.

MARSHAL DILL observed, with regard to General Marshall's draft, that the restrictions on the commander were too great; that the proposition formed a good basis to work on, but the restrictions would make it very difficult for the Commander-in-Chief to exercise command.

GENERAL MARSHALL agreed that the restrictions were great, but stated that if the Supreme Commander ended up with no more authority than to tell Washington what he wanted, such a situation was better than nothing, and an improvement over the present situation.

AIR CHIEF MARSHAL PORTAL commended the paper for its realism; he observed that it separated a commander's resources in air defense and air offense, which indicated some of the problems of such a proposition. He stated that the primary consideration should be what is sound from a military point of view; that what might be gained by the military aspect of unified command might be lost by the necessity of political considerations. He asked if it would not be possible to give the commander a free hand, and to have all the political questions resolved, say, in Washington, or, as an alternative suggestion, by a representative in the area, rather along the lines adopted by the British in the Middle East.

GENERAL MARSHALL said that political questions could be settled in Washington. He agreed that his paper had been drawn on realistic lines. He thought Air Marshal Portal was talking more in terms of idealism; that what he desired to do was to start something.

ADMIRAL STARK pointed out that under the provisions of the draft directive, troops of one nation could not be moved out of its own possessions without approval of the home government. He felt that the restrictions were heavy, but realistic; and that it was better to have restrictions first and then remove them, than to fail in establishing the principle.

AIR MARSHAL PORTAL pointed out that if the Supreme Commander desired to move the air forces of one of the elements of the command, he should know the capabilities of these forces, and that could only be accomplished by having a suitable liaison element.

ADMIRAL KING thought that it would be impossible to get the idea of a single Commander-in-Chief accepted by the governments concerned unless the limitations were imposed. He suggested that the Chiefs of Staff Conference prepare an outline plan for presentation to the Prime Minister and the President.

U. S. SECRET
BRITISH MOST SECRET

ADMIRAL POUND stated that he realized the urgency of coming to a decision in the matter, whatever it might be; and asked, on the assumption that unified command was recommended, how would the many details be worked out? He pointed out that there are a large number of details involved. He thought that it would be difficult to keep the staff of the Commander-in-Chief small for he would have to have representatives of the services of each nation to advise him. The British Chiefs of Staff agreed as to the urgency of getting to a conclusion on the question immediately.

During the discussion it was suggested that the broad outline be prepared and the details worked out later.

6. UTILIZATION OF THE U. S. TRANSPORTS NOW BEING USED IN THE INDIAN OCEAN.

ADMIRAL POUND said that it might prove advantageous to the general scheme for reinforcing the Far East if these transports, when they had delivered the 18th British Division at its destination, could be used for carrying additional reinforcements from the Middle East to the Far East. He asked whether such a proposal would be approved by the United States Chiefs of Staff.

ADMIRAL STARK said that these ships would be available for use as seemed best in the joint cause.

ADMIRAL POUND said that he did not ask for an immediate decision in the matter, but thought it best to draw attention to the possibility that such a request might be made.

The Conference adjourned at 4:30 p.m.

ENCLOSURE
   Annex 1 - Draft of Instructions
          to the Supreme Commander,
          Southwestern Pacific
          Theater.

ANNEX 1

TO

JCCSs-4

U. S. SECRET
BRITISH MOST SECRET

ABC-4   Proposed draft of instructions to the
C/S USA   Supreme Commander, Southwestern Pacific
                Theater, submitted by United States Chiefs
                of Staff for the consideration of the Joint
                United States-British Chiefs of Staff Conference.

      Letter of Instructions to be signed by the government of the country from which the Supreme Commander is chosen, and countersigned by representatives of each of the other powers in the group, Australia, Dutch East Indies, British and the United States.

To: Supreme Commander, Southwestern Pacific Theater.

            (Letters, similar in content, will be sent by
            each of the ADBU governments to its highest
            Army, Navy and Air Commander in the Southwestern
            Pacific Theater.)

Subject: Letter of Instructions.

     1. By agreement among the Governments of Australia, The Netherlands, the United Kingdom and the United States, hereinafter referred to as the ADBU governments, the Southwestern Pacific Theater has been constituted, to comprise all land and sea areas included in the region Malaya - Australia - Philippine Islands, all inclusive.

     2. You have been designated as the Supreme Commander of the Southwestern Theater and of all armed forces afloat, ashore and in the air of the ADBU governments stationed therein and allotted by their respective governments for service in that theater, except that you are not authorized to transfer from the territory of any of the ADBU governments land troops of that government except with the consent of the local commander or his government. You are authorized to employ naval and air forces in general support of operations in the theater assigned you. However, during the period of initial air reinforcement, it being the view of all the associated governments that air superiority over the enemy should be attained as soon as possible, each government reserves the right to assign and employ its pursuit and fighter airplanes at its own discretion. All accumulations of pursuit and fighter airplanes beyond the minimum requirements fixed by each government, will pass to your general reserve, for use under your direction.

     3. The ADBU governments have further agreed as follows:

U. S. SECRET
BRITISH MOST SECRET

    <u>a</u>.   The mission of the armed forces in the Southwestern Pacific is immediately to:

    (1)   Prevent further Japanese penetration of the Southwestern Pacific Theater.

    (2)   Establish security of essential land, air and sea communications within the theater. At this time essential communications in the Southwest Pacific theater are:

    (a)   The approaches from India and to East Australia; and

    (b)   Extending from such approaches to Singapore, and, through the Dutch East Indies, to the Philippines.

    (3)   Eventually defeat the Japanese forces in the theater and expel them therefrom.

    <u>b</u>.   Your duties, responsibilities and authority are defined as follows:

    (1)   To coordinate in Southwestern Pacific theater the tactical and strategic operations of all armed forces of the ADBU governments to assign them strategic and/or tactical missions and objectives, and, where desirable, to organize task forces for the execution of specific operations.

    (2)   To submit recommendations to the Associated Governments in all matters pertaining to that theater, regarding which specific authority is not herein delegated to you.

    (3)   To require, from the Commanders of the Armed Forces of each of the ADBU governments, such reports as you deem necessary in the determination of tactical strength and effectiveness, and/or in the discharge of your responsibilities as Supreme Commander.

    <u>c</u>.   The following specific limitations are placed by the ADBU governments upon your authority as Supreme Commander, Southwestern Pacific Theater:

    (1)   You may not relieve from duty the Commander of any of the Armed Forces of any of the ADBU governments, or any subordinate of such commander.

    (2)   You may not destroy, revise or alter the major tactical organization of the armed forces of any ADBU government. Each national component of a task force will operate under its own commander

U. S. SECRET
BRITISH MOST SECRET

and will not be distributed into small units attached to the other national components of the task force.

(3) You may not take over for general use the supplies, munitions or other material resources belonging to any one of the ADBU governments without the consent of the appropriate commander, nor may you interfere in the administrative and/or disciplinary control of such Commander over his own forces.

(4) You may not prevent or interfere in direct communication between the Commander of the Armed Forces of any one of the ADBU governments with his home government.

(5) You may not prevent the Commander of the Armed Forces of any ADBU government from obeying the orders of his own government in detaching troops, individuals or material to any other theater.

(6) You may not assume direct command of any portion or part of the forces assigned to the theater or of any particular portion or section of such theater, but will exercise your authority through the duly designated commanders of the ADBU governments.

(7) You may not, at any time, locate your headquarters within the limits of any critical tactical zone, but will so situate such headquarters as to facilitate establishment and maintenance of communications with all tactical zones and so as to provide you with a balanced perspective of the complete theater.

4. The ADBU governments have also agreed that they will jointly and severally support you in the execution of the duties and responsibilities as above defined, and in the exercise of the authority as above defined, and in the exercise of the authority as above delegated and limited. Commanders of all naval, air and ground forces within your theater will be immediately informed by their respective governments that all orders and instructions issued by you in conformity with the provisions of this letter will be considered by such commanders as emanating from their respective governments.

No government will materially reduce its armed forces assigned to your theater nor any commitments made by it for reinforcing its forces in your theater except after giving to the other governments, and to you, timely information pertaining thereto.

5. As Supreme Commander of the Southwestern Pacific Theater, you are directly responsible to this government, and all instructions to you will follow established methods. Any recommendation, report, request, or other communication between you and any of the other governments of the ADBU Powers will be processed through this government.

U. S. SECRET
BRITISH MOST SECRET

    6.   Your headquarters will be established, initially, in Java.

                                                            Signed

                                                  (By Power furnishing
                                                     Supreme Commander)

Countersigned:

    Other ADBU representatives.

U. S. SECRET
BRITISH MOST SECRET

ABC-4
JCCSs-5

THE CHIEFS OF STAFF CONFERENCE

FEDERAL RESERVE BUILDING

WASHINGTON, D. C.

4 P.M., DECEMBER 29, 1941

Present

British Officers

    Admiral of the Fleet, Sir Dudley Pound, First Sea Lord and Chief of Naval Staff
    Field Marshal Sir John Dill
    Admiral Sir Charles Little, Joint Staff Mission
    Lieut. General Sir Colville Wemyss, Joint Staff Mission
    Air Marshal A. T. Harris, Joint Staff Mission

U. S. Naval Officers

    Admiral H. R. Stark, Chief of Naval Operations
    Admiral E. J. King, Commander-in-Chief, U. S. Fleet
    Rear Admiral W. R. Sexton, President, General Board
    Rear Admiral F. J. Horne, Assistant Chief, Naval Operations
    Rear Admiral J. H. Towers, Chief, Bureau of Aeronautics
    Rear Admiral R. K. Turner, Director, War Plans Division
    Major General Thomas Holcomb, Commandant, U. S. Marine Corps
    Lieut. Commander R. E. Libby, U. S. Navy

U. S. Army Officers

    General George C. Marshall, Commanding General of the Field Forces and Chief of Staff
    Lieut. General H. H. Arnold, Chief of Army Air Forces and Deputy Chief of Staff
    Brigadier General Raymond Lee, Acting Assistant Chief of Staff, G-2, War Department

U. S. SECRET
BRITISH MOST SECRET

Joint Secretaries

    Colonel E. I. C. Jacob
    Commander R. D. Coleridge, R.N.
    Captain J. L. McCrea, Aide to Chief of Naval Operations
    Lieut. Colonel P. M. Robinett, G-2, GHQ, U. S. Army
    Major W. T. Sexton, Assistant Secretary, W.D.G.S.

1. PRIORITIES FOR UNITED STATES AND UNITED KINGDOM OVERSEAS EXPEDITIONS IN THE ATLANTIC OCEAN.

THE CONFERENCE approved a final draft of the Joint Planning Committee's Report on Priorities for United States and United Kingdom Overseas Expeditions in the Atlantic Ocean. (U. S. Serial ABC-4/1, British Serial WW (J.P.C.)1). (See Annex 1)

2. AMERICAN-BRITISH STRATEGY (WW-1).

At the request of REAR ADMIRAL TURNER, action on this paper was deferred.

3. NORTHWEST AFRICA PROJECT, U. S. ABC-4/2, BRITISH WW(J.P.C.)2.

Action on this paper was deferred at the request of the British.

4. SUPPORTING MEASURES FOR THE SOUTHWEST PACIFIC.

Action on U. S. ABC-4/3, British WW(J.P.C.)3, was deferred by common consent.

At this time, the following officers withdrew from the Conference: Rear Admiral W. R. Sexton, U. S. N.; Rear Admiral R. K. Turner, U. S. N.; Rear Admiral J. H. Towers, U. S. N.; Major General Thomas Holcomb, U. S. M. C.; Captain J. L. McCrea, U. S. N.; Brigadier General Raymond Lee, U. S. A.; and Commander R. D. Coleridge, R. N.

5. UNITY OF COMMAND IN THE SOUTHWESTERN PACIFIC THEATER.

    a METHOD OF HANDLING QUESTIONS CONCERNING THAT THEATER.

ADMIRAL POUND said that the proposal for the establishment of unity of command in the Southwestern Pacific Theater had been referred by the Prime Minister to London, for consideration by the War Cabinet. In his telegram he had included the following sentence, "He (General Wavell) would receive his orders from an appropriate joint body, who will be responsible to him as Minister of Defense, and to the President of the United States, who is also Commander-in-Chief of all U. S. forces."

U. S. SECRET
BRITISH MOST SECRET

The Prime Minister had received an immediate reply, asking for information as to the nature of this joint body. He had been asked to defer giving his views to London on this point until the Chiefs of Staff had had an opportunity of putting forward their views.

One of the main objects in setting up a Supreme Commander was to achieve rapidity of decision on important matters. It would be difficult to attain this object if a cumbersome machine were erected to deal with important matters arising from the Southwestern Pacific Theater. The right course would be to utilize existing machinery, and the British Chiefs of Staff had formulated certain proposals which they hoped would prove acceptable to the United States Chiefs of Staff.

ADMIRAL POUND then read his proposals to the Conference. (See Annex 2).

ADMIRAL KING said that he had been asked to consider this matter, and advise the President at very short notice. He had set down on paper an outline of a solution which he thought would achieve the object in view, namely, rapid decision through the use of existing machinery. His proposal was that the Prime Minister should appoint a deputy in Washington, who would act with the President on recommendations to be made by a Southwestern Pacific Council, which would be a military body composed of one representative from each of the following:- U. S. Joint Board, the British Joint Staff Mission, the Dutch military representatives in Washington, together with one Anzac representative. The members of this Council would be instructed as necessary by the military bodies which they represented.

GENERAL MARSHALL suggested that it might be better not to introduce at this stage the complicated question of machinery into the business of setting up unity of command. He thought that an amendment might be made to the documents establishing the unified command, which would include a phrase to the effect that "matters would be dealt with by such joint machinery as the Associated Powers may hereafter set up".

ADMIRAL KING thought that the establishment of machinery was an indispensable part of the establishment of unity of command, if the latter were to start operating at once.

GENERAL MARSHALL said that if such were the case, he was prepared to accept the proposals put forward by the British Chiefs of Staff.

ADMIRAL KING and ADMIRAL STARK signified their agreement to these proposals.

ADMIRAL HORNE suggested that in order to achieve unity of command without delay, it should be agreed upon and established by the

U. S. SECRET
BRITISH MOST SECRET

British and United States Governments forthwith -- the other Governments concerned being presented with a fait accompli, and being asked to notify their acceptance.

ADMIRAL POUND said that the Prime Minister had already sent off telegrams to the New Zealand and Australian Governments, so that there was unlikely to be much delay. The British Chiefs of Staff proposed to telegraph their proposals to the Prime Minister forthwith for his approval.

ADMIRAL STARK said that he would also submit them forthwith to the President.

> The United States and British Chiefs of Staff approved the proposals for handling matters concerning the Southwestern Pacific Theater, as set out in the Memorandum as Annex 2, and agreed to submit them forthwith to the President and the Prime Minister, for approval.

b LETTER OF INSTRUCTIONS TO THE SUPREME COMMANDER.

THE CONFERENCE was informed that a draft Letter of Instructions, prepared by the Joint Planning Committee, would be circulated to them that evening. The British Chiefs of Staff proposed to telegraph its contents to London for comment.

> THE CONFERENCE took note of this, and agreed to meet at 11:30 the following morning to consider the Draft Letter.

6. PROPOSED COMMUNICATION TO GENERALISSIMO CHIANG KAI-SHEK.

GENERAL MARSHALL said that the President was very anxious to send a message to Generalissimo Chiang Kai-Shek, so as to reach him before the public announcement of the setting up of unified command in the Southwestern Pacific Theater. General Magruder had reported that the Generalissimo was considerably upset by events in Burma, and particularly by the diversion to the British there of Lend-Lease materiel destined for China. It would therefore be desirable to send him an encouraging message, which would make clear that the other Associated Powers considered that he had an important part to play on the world's stage. This would obviate any danger which might exist of his resenting the fact that he had not been consulted about the setting up of the Southwestern Pacific Command. He (General Marshall) had accordingly drafted a message, which he read to the Conference.

U. S. SECRET
BRITISH MOST SECRET

     In the course of discussion, two minor amendments were agreed to, to meet the following points:

     <u>a</u> That it would be unwise to define at this stage the Southwestern Pacific Theater.

     <u>b</u> That in view of the controversial problem presented by Burma, it would be inadvisable to include any part of Burma in the Chinese theater. It would be best, in defining the latter theater, to make clear that it was an initial definition only.

> The United States and British Chiefs of Staff approved the draft message to Generalissimo Chiang Kai-Shek, as amended in discussion, and agreed to submit it to the President and to the Prime Minister, for their approval. (See Annex 3).

     The Conference adjourned at 5:30 P.M. to meet at 11:30 A.M., December 30, 1941.

ENCLOSURES:

    Annex 1 - Priorities for United States and United Kingdom Overseas Expeditions in the Atlantic Ocean (U. S. ABC-4/1 - British WW-5)
    Annex 2 Proposed Method of Handling Matters Concerning the Southwest Pacific Theater.
    Annex 3 - Proposed Message to Chiang Kai-Shek.

U. S. SECRET
BRITISH MOST SECRET

U. S. ABC-4/1
BRITISH WW-5   December 29, 1941

ANNEX 1
to
JCCSs-5

UNITED STATES - BRITISH

CHIEFS OF STAFF

APPROVED

REPORT BY THE U. S. - BRITISH JOINT
PLANNING COMMITTEE
U.S. ABC-4/1, BRITISH WW(JPC)1

PRIORITIES FOR UNITED STATES AND

UNITED KINGDOM OVERSEAS EXPEDITIONS

IN THE ATLANTIC OCEAN

U. S. SECRET
BRITISH MOST SECRET

U. S. SERIAL ABC-4/1
BRITISH SERIAL WW(J.P.C.) 1

PRIORITIES FOR UNITED STATES AND UNITED KINGDOM OVERSEAS EXPEDITIONS IN THE ATLANTIC OCEAN

REPORT BY THE U. S. - BRITISH JOINT PLANNING COMMITTEE

1. One of the directives to the Joint Planning Committee issued by the Chiefs of Staff Committee on December 24, 1941, may be summarized as follows:-

Study and report outline plans for the overseas employment of United States and British troops in the Atlantic region, indicating recommended relative priorities of importance:

    a   The relief by United States troops of British troops in Iceland and North Ireland.

    b   The occupation by invitation of the following positions:

        (1) The Azores.
        (2) The Cape Verde Islands.
        (3) The Canary Islands.
        (4) French West Africa.
        (5) French North Africa.
        (6) Diego Suarez in Madagascar.
        (7) Curacao and Aruba.
        (8) Northeast Brazil.

2. The Joint Planning Committee recommends that the initial occupation by invitation of the foreign positions indicated in the directive should be allocated as follows:

    a   To the United States - the occupation of the Cape Verde Islands, French West Africa, Curacao and Aruba, Northeast Brazil.

    b   To the United Kingdom - the occupation of the Azores, the Canary Islands, and Diego Suarez in Madagascar.

    c   To the United States and the United Kingdom acting jointly - the occupation of French North Africa.

U. S. SECRET
BRITISH MOST SECRET

    3.   If the operation in French North Africa as submitted in our plan (U. S. Serial ABC-4/2, British Serial WW) is undertaken, we see no prospect of any other major movements being carried out in the Atlantic area for at least three months, and normal reinforcements to the eastward from the United Kingdom will be severely curtailed. The reason is lack of an adequate amount of troop transport, in view of the heavy reinforcements being sent to Hawaii, Samoa, and Australia, and requirements for the continuous support of outlying United States and United Kingdom field armies, garrisons, and naval forces. Furthermore, minimum requirements for naval protection of new lines of naval communications will seriously reduce the protection now being afforded the trade routes in the Atlantic and Indian Oceans.

    4.   No major overseas operations can be performed by the United States unless adequate shipping is immediately made available for preparation as troop transports.

U. S. SECRET
BRITISH MOST SECRET   December 29, 1941

ANNEX 2
to
JCCSs-5

PROPOSED METHOD OF HANDLING MATTERS

CONCERNING THE SOUTHWEST PACIFIC THEATER

1. It is assumed that the chief matters on which decisions would have to be given would be:

    <u>a</u>   The provision of reinforcements.
    <u>b</u>   A major change in policy.
    <u>c</u>   Departure from the Supreme Commander's directive.

2. It is suggested that no special body should be set up for this purpose because it would tend to clog the machine for the following reasons:

    <u>a</u>   It would be necessary to have Dutch, Australian, and New Zealand representatives on this body.

    <u>b</u>   Each representative in <u>a</u> would probably wish for time to consult his government before giving an opinion.

3. It is proposed, therefore, that existing machinery should be used in the following manner:

    <u>a</u>   The Supreme Commander would telegraph to the Chiefs of Staff Committee, both in London and in Washington, his proposal, whatever it might be.

    <u>b</u>   The Chiefs of Staff Committee in London would immediately telegraph to the British Mission in Washington to say whether or not they would be telegraphing any opinions.

    <u>c</u>   On receipt of these opinions, the United States Chiefs of Staff and the Representatives in Washington of the British Chiefs of Staff would meet and consider the problem and would submit their recommendations to the President and by telegraph to the Prime Minister and Minister of Defence. The Prime Minister would then inform the President whether he was in agreement with their recommendations.

4. As the Dutch Government is in London, and as the principal representatives of the New Zealand and Australian Governments are also in London, it is proposed that the agreement of these Governments to any proposal should be obtained by the British Government and this would be included in the final telegram to Washington.

U. S. SECRET
BRITISH MOST SECRET

5. Agreement having been reached between London and Washington, the orders to the Supreme Commander would then be dispatched from Washington.

U. S. SECRET
BRITISH MOST SECRET

December 29, 1941

ANNEX 3
to
JCCSs-5

MEMORANDUM FOR THE PRESIDENT:

It is suggested that as soon as a preliminary decision is reached as to the delimitation of the Southwest Pacific theater, and in agreement with the British and Dutch authorities, a communication in substance as follows be dispatched to Chiang Kai-Shek:

1. In order to insure immediate coordination and cooperation in our common effort against the enemy, there is being established a Supreme Commander for all British, Dutch, and American forces in the Southwest Pacific theater.

2. The advisability of a similar command of activities of the Associated Powers in the Chinese theater appears evident. This theater we suggest should initially include such portion of Thailand and Indo-China as may become accessible to troops of the Associated Powers. In agreement with the representatives of the British and Dutch Governments, I desire to suggest that you should undertake to exercise such command over all forces of the Associated Powers which are now, or may in the future be operating in the Chinese theater.

3. It is our thought that, in order to make such command effective, a joint planning staff should at once be organized consisting of representatives of the British, Dutch, American, and Chinese governments. If you consider it practicable, and Russia agrees, a Russian representative might be included. This staff should function under your supreme command.

4. The commander of the Southwest Pacific theater and the commander of the British forces in India would be directed to maintain the closest liaison with your headquarters. A mutual exchange of liaison officers between the three headquarters would be desirable.

5. Such arrangements would enable your counsel and influence to be given effect in the formulation of the general strategy for the conduct of the war in all theaters. Your views in this matter will be greatly appreciated by me.

U. S. SECRET
BRITISH MOST SECRET

ABC-4
JCCSs-6

THE CHIEFS OF STAFF CONFERENCE

FEDERAL RESERVE BUILDING

WASHINGTON, D. C.

3 P.M., DECEMBER 30, 1941.

Present

British Officers

　Navy

　　Admiral of the Fleet, Sir Dudley Pound, First Sea Lord and Chief of
　　　　Naval Staff
　　Admiral Sir Charles Little, Joint Staff Mission
　　Captain Charles E. Lambe, R.N., Deputy Director of Plans, Admiralty

　Army

　　Field Marshal Sir John Dill
　　Lieut. General Sir Colville Wemyss, Joint Staff Mission
　　Brigadier V. Dykes, Director of Plans, War Office

　Air Force

　　Air Marshal A. T. Harris, Joint Staff Mission
　　Air Commodore W. F. Dickson, Director of Plans, Air Ministry

United States Officers

　Navy

　　Admiral H. R. Stark, Chief of Naval Operations (Presiding)
　　Admiral E. J. King, Commander-in-Chief, U. S. Fleet
　　Rear Admiral W. R. Sexton, President, General Board
　　Rear Admiral F. J. Horne, Assistant to the Chief of Naval Operations
　　Rear Admiral J. H. Towers, Chief of Bureau of Aeronautics
　　Rear Admiral R. K. Turner, Director, War Plans Division
　　Major General Thomas Holcomb, Major General Commandant, U.S.M.C.
　　Lieut. Commander R. E. Libby, Aide to Admiral E. J. King.

U. S. SECRET
BRITISH MOST SECRET

Army

    General G. C. Marshall, Commanding General of the Field Forces
        and Chief of Staff
    Lieut. General H. H. Arnold, Chief of Army Air Forces and Deputy
        Chief of Staff
    Brigadier General Raymond Lee, Acting Assistant Chief of Staff, G-2
    Brigadier General L. T. Gerow, Assistant Chief of Staff, WPD
    Brigadier General D. D. Eisenhower, G.S.C.

Joint Secretaries

    Colonel E. I. C. Jacob
    Commander R. D. Coleridge, R.N.
    Captain J. L. McCrea, Aide to the Chief of Naval Operations
    Lt. Col. P. M. Robinett, G-2, GHQ, U.S.A.
    Major W. T. Sexton, Assistant Secretary, W.D.G.S.

1. HIGHER DIRECTION OF WAR IN THE ABDA AREA. -

THE COMMITTEE gave further consideration to their Memorandum on the Higher Direction of War in the ABDA Area, which had been telegraphed to Ottawa, and had received the approval of the Prime Minister, together with a redraft of this paper, which had been forwarded by Mr. Hopkins for their attention, (Annex 1, Memorandum of Mr. Hopkins, December 30, 1941.)

In the course of discussion, the following points were made: -

    a. It did not appear desirable to set up a special body to deal with ABDA problems, as only the United States Chiefs of Staff and the British Chiefs of Staff, through their representatives in Washington, could weigh the needs of the ABDA Area in relation to those of other theatres.

    b. As the Dutch Government was in London, and as the machinery for consultation with the Dominions Governments already existed there, it seemed proper that consultation with these Governments should take place in London, and that the British Government should be responsible for obtaining the views and agreements of these Governments, and for submitting them to the United States Chiefs of Staff and the representatives in Washington of the British Chiefs of Staff. While the representatives of the Dutch and Dominions Governments in Washington could, if thought desirable, be kept informed of developments, official consultation could only take place in London.

U. S. SECRET
BRITISH MOST SECRET

    c. In order to avoid delay, communications from the Supreme Commander should be telegraphed to London and Washington simultaneously -- the telegram for Washington being for action, and that to London to furnish a basis for immediate comment to Washington.

  In view of the above considerations, it was felt that while some of the suggestions in the redraft forwarded by Mr. Hopkins could be accepted, the main principles contained in their original Memorandum should be retained. The Committee accordingly prepared a revised version of their Memorandum, in two parts. (See Annex 2).

  The United States and British Chiefs of Staff agreed that the revised Memorandum on the Higher Direction of War in the ABDA Area should be submitted to the President for his approval under a covering Memorandum setting out the reasons for the machinery proposed.

  2.   DRAFT DIRECTIVE TO THE SUPREME COMMANDER IN THE ABDA AREA. -

  The Committee had before them a Report by the Joint Planning Committee (U.S. ABC-4/5, British WW (J.P.C.)5).

  Discussion took place on the extent of the ABDA Area.

  ADMIRAL STARK reminded the Committee that a telegram had been sent to Generalissimo Chiang Kai-Shek, in which it had been suggested that Indo-China and Thailand should be included in the Chinese theatre, and his comments on this arrangement had been requested. He felt, therefore, that, for political reasons, it would be necessary to exclude Indo-China and Thailand from the ABDA Area.

  ADMIRAL POUND and MARSHAL DILL agreed with this view, and explained that they felt that Burma should be included in the ABDA Area as an essential supply route to China. Burma had recently been transferred from the Far Eastern Command to the Indian Command, as being an important outpost of the Indian defense, but the British Chiefs of Staff now agreed that it should be included in the ABDA Area.

  THE BRITISH CHIEFS OF STAFF agreed to a proposal put forward by the United States Chiefs of Staff that a paragraph should be included to the effect that the Deputy Supreme Commander and, if required, a Commander of the combined Naval forces, should be jointly designated by the ABDA Governments.

  THE UNITED STATES AND BRITISH CHIEFS OF STAFF accepted the Draft Directive to the Supreme Commander in the ABDA Area, as amended by the Committee, and including the Memorandum on the Higher Direction of War in the ABDA Area (Annex 2 to the Report), as an agreed report, for submission to the President and the Prime Minister. (See Annex 3, U.S. ABC-4/5, British WW 3,-December 30, 1941).

U. S. SECRET
BRITISH MOST SECRET

    3.   NEXT MEETING. -

The United States and British Chiefs of Staff agreed to meet at 2 p.m. the following day, Wednesday, December 31, 1941, to consider two reports by the Joint Planning Committee: -

        a. Northwest Africa Project.

           (U.S. ABC-4/2; British WW (J.P.C.)2).

        b. Supporting Measures for the Southwestern Pacific.

           (U.S. ABC-4/3; British WW (J.P.C.)3).

ENCLOSURES:

    Annex 1 - Memorandum from Mr. Hopkins December 30, 1941.
    Annex 2 - Memorandum for the President, Higher Direction of War in
                ABDA Area (in 2 Parts).
    Annex 3 - Draft Directive to Supreme Commander in ABDA Area, US ABC-
                4/5, British WW-3 (with 2 Annexes).

U. S. SECRET
BRITISH MOST SECRET

ANNEX 1
to
JCCSs-6

The White House
Washington

December 30, 1941.

Dear Betty:

     Here is the re-draft which the President did last night and which he would like to have the Joint Staffs chew over.

               Cordially yours,

                  /s/ HARRY L. HOPKINS

Enclosure.

Admiral Harold R. Stark,
    Chief of Naval Operations,
        Navy Department.

* * * * * * *

PROPOSED METHOD OF HANDLING MATTERS CONCERNING THE SOUTHWEST PACIFIC THEATRE.

1. It is assumed that the chief matters on which decisions would have to be given would be:

    a. The provision of reinforcements.
    b. A major change in policy.
    c. Departure from the Supreme Commander's directive.

2. It is suggested that a special body be set up for this purpose in Washington.

    a. Three Americans and three British.
    b. One Australian, one New Zealander and one Dutch, for consultation and advisory purposes.

3. It is proposed, therefore, that the above machinery should be used in the following manner:

U. S. SECRET
BRITISH MOST SECRET

    a. The Supreme Commander would telegraph to the above Committee in Washington, his proposal, whatever it might be.
    b. The Committee in Washington would immediately telegraph to London to ask for any recommendations or opinions.
    c. On receipt of these opinions, the Washington Committee would submit their recommendations to the President, and by telegraph to the Prime Minister. The Prime Minister would then inform the President whether he was in agreement with their recommendations. He could of course consult with Australia, New Zealand, and The Netherlands if advisable.

4. Agreement, having been reached between the Prime Minister, and the President, the orders to the Supreme Commander would then be dispatched from Washington in the name of both of them.

U S   SECRET
BRITISH MOST SECRET

Part I

ANNEX 2
to
JCCSs-6

December 30, 1941

MEMORANDUM FOR THE PRESIDENT:

HIGHER DIRECTION OF WAR IN THE ABDA AREA

      The Chiefs of Staff have somewhat revised their original memorandum on the above subject, so as to incorporate certain of the President's suggestions. With respect to those points where the revised memorandum, hereto attached, differs from the President's re-draft, the following explanation is submitted:

    a. The United States Chiefs of Staff and the British Chiefs of Staff, through their representatives in Washington, are in an especially favorable position to weigh the needs of the ABDA area in relation to those of other theaters of war. Recommendations to the President and to the Prime Minister emanating from the joint Chiefs of Staff would reflect this balanced perspective.

    b. Consultations with the Dutch, Australian, and New Zealand governments can not well be carried out in several places without serious loss of time, and creation of confusion. For the reasons set out in paragraph 4 of the attached revised memorandum, London would appear to be the logical place for carrying on such consultations. The Chiefs of Staff committee in Washington can, of course, keep the representatives of the Dutch and Dominion governments informed, should this be considered desirable.

    c. The suggested duplication of messages from the Supreme Commander to London and Washington is for the purpose of saving time. The copy sent to Washington would be the action copy, but the one to London would furnish the basis for immediate comment to Washington.

    d. Admiral Pound feels that, in view of his conversation with the Prime Minister this morning, the attached procedure will be entirely acceptable to the Prime Minister.

Chief of Staff   Chief of Naval Operations

Commander-in-Chief   Chief of Air Forces
U S Fleet

U. S. SECRET
BRITISH MOST SECRET

PART II

ANNEX 2
to
JCCSs-6

December 30, 1941

HIGHER DIRECTION OF WAR IN THE ABDA AREA

1. On all important military matters, not within the jurisdiction of the Supreme Commander of the ABDA Area, the U. S. Chiefs of Staff and the representatives in Washington of the British Chiefs of Staff will constitute the agency for developing and submitting recommendations for decision by the President of the United States and by the British Prime Minister and Minister of Defense. Among the chief matters on which decisions will be required are:

   a. The provision of reinforcements.
   b. A major change in policy.
   c. Departure from the Supreme Commander's directive.

2. This agency will function as follows:

   a. Any proposal coming either from the Supreme Commander or from any of the ABDA governments will be transmitted to the Chiefs of Staff Committee both in Washington and in London.

   b. The Chiefs of Staff Committee in London will immediately telegraph to their representatives in Washington to say whether or not they will be telegraphing any opinions.

   c. On receipt of these opinions, the United States Chiefs of Staff and the representatives in Washington of the British Chiefs of Staff will develop and submit their recommendations to the President, and by telegraph to the Prime Minister and Minister of Defense. The Prime Minister will then inform the President whether he is in agreement with these recommendations.

3. Since London has the machinery for consulting the Dominion Governments, and since the Dutch Government is in London, the British Government will be responsible for obtaining their views and agreement, and for including these in the final telegram to Washington.

4. Agreement having been reached between the President and the Prime Minister and Minister of Defense, the orders to the Supreme Commander will be dispatched from Washington in the name of both of them.

U. S. SECRET
BRITISH MOST SECRET

ANNEX 3
to
JCCSs-6

December 30, 1941

U.S. ABC-4/5
BRITISH WW-3

REPORT

By

UNITED STATES - BRITISH

CHIEFS OF STAFF

DRAFT DIRECTIVE TO THE SUPREME

COMMANDER IN THE ABDA AREA

U. S. SECRET
BRITISH MOST SECRET

December 30, 1941

U.S. SERIAL ABC-4/5
BRITISH SERIAL WW-3

ANNEX 3
to
JCCSs-6

BY AGREEMENT AMONG THE GOVERNMENTS OF

AUSTRALIA, THE NETHERLANDS, THE UNITED

KINGDOM AND THE UNITED STATES, HEREINAFTER

REFERRED TO AS THE ABDA GOVERNMENTS:

1. AREA. -

A strategic area has been constituted, to comprise initially all land and sea areas included in the general region Burma - Malaya - Netherlands East Indies and the Philippines; more precisely defined in Annex 1. This area will be known as the ABDA Area.

2. FORCES. -

You have been designated as the Supreme Commander of the ABDA Area and of all armed forces, afloat, ashore and in the air, of the ABDA Governments which are:

    a. Stationed in the Area;

    b. Located in Australian territory when such forces have been allotted by the respective governments for services in or in support of the ABDA Area

You are not authorized to transfer from the territory of any of the ABDA Governments, land forces of that government without the consent of the local commander or his government.

3. The Deputy Supreme Commander and/or, if required, a commander of the combined naval forces and a commander of the combined air forces will be jointly designated by the ABDA Governments.

4. No government will materially reduce its armed forces assigned to your Area nor any commitments made by it for reinforcing its forces in your Area except after giving to the other governments, and to you, timely information pertaining thereto.

U. S. SECRET
BRITISH MOST SECRET

5. STRATEGIC CONCEPT AND POLICY. -

The basic strategic concept of the ABDA Governments for the conduct of the war in your Area is to maintain initially the strategic defensive. The ABDA Governments intend to provide immediate reinforcements for defense. As additional forces become available, it will become possible to take the offensive and ultimately to conduct an all-out offensive against Japan. The first essential is to gain general air superiority at the earliest possible moment, through the employment of concentrated air power. The piecemeal employment of air forces should be minimized. Although your operations in the near future must be primarily for defense, they should be so conducted as to further preparations for that offensive.

6. THE GENERAL STRATEGIC POLICY WILL THEREFORE BE:-

a. To hold the Malay Barrier as the basic defensive position of the ABDA Area, and to operate air and sea forces in as great depth as possible forward of the Barrier in order to oppose the Japanese southward advance.

b. To hold Burma and Australia as essential supporting positions for the Area, and Burma as essential to the support of China, and to the defense of India.

c. To re-establish communications through the Dutch East Indies with Luzon, and to support the Philippines' Garrison.

d. To maintain essential communications within the Area.

7. DUTIES, RESPONSIBILITIES AND AUTHORITY OF THE SUPREME COMMANDER. -

You will coordinate in the ABDA Area the strategic operations of all armed forces of the ABDA Governments; assign them strategic missions and objectives; where desirable, arrange for the formation of task forces, whether national or international, for the execution of specific operations; and appoint any officer, irrespective of seniority or nationality, to command such task forces.

8. While you will have no responsibilities in respect of the internal administration of the respective forces under your command, you are authorized to direct and coordinate the creation and development of administrative facilities and the broad allocation of war materials.

9. You will dispose reinforcements which from time to time may be dispatched to the Area by the ABDA Governments.

U. S. SECRET
BRITISH MOST SECRET

10. You are authorized to require from the commanders of the armed forces under your command such reports as you deem necessary in the discharge of your responsibilities as Supreme Commander.

11. You are authorized to control the issue of all communiques concerning the forces under your command.

12. Through the channels specified in paragraph 18, you may submit recommendations to the ABDA Governments on any matters pertaining to the furtherance of your mission.

13. LIMITATIONS. -

Your authority and control with respect to the various portions of the ABDA Area and to the forces assigned thereto will normally be exercised through the commanders duly designated by their respective governments. Interference is to be avoided in the administrative processes of the armed forces of any of the ABDA Governments, including free communication between them and their respective governments. No alteration or revision is to be made in the basic tactical organization of such forces, and each national component of a task force will normally operate under its own commander and will not be subdivided into small units for attachment to the other national components of the task force. In general, your instructions and orders will be limited to those necessary for effective coordination of forces in the execution of your mission.

14. RELATIONS WITH ABDA GOVERNMENTS. -

The ABDA Governments will jointly and severally support you in the execution of the duties and responsibilities as herein defined, and in the exercise of the authority herein delegated and limited. Commanders of all sea, land and air forces within your Area will be immediately informed by their respective governments that, from a date to be notified, all orders and instructions issued by you in conformity with the provisions of this directive will be considered by such commanders as emanating from their respective governments.

15. If any of your immediate subordinates, after making due representations to you, still considers that obedience to your orders would jeopardize the national interests of his country to an extent unjustified by the general situation in the ABDA Area, he has the right, subject to your being immediately notified of such intention, to appeal direct to his own government before carrying out the orders. Such appeals will be made by the most expeditious method and a copy of the appeal will be communicated simultaneously to you.

U. S. SECRET
BRITISH MOST SECRET

16. STAFF AND ASSUMPTION OF COMMAND. -

Your staff will include officers of each of the ABDA powers. You are empowered to communicate immediately with the national commanders in the Area with a view to obtaining staff officers essential to your earliest possible assumption of command. Your additional staff requirements will be communicated as soon as possible to the ABDA Governments through channels of communication described in Paragraph 18.

17. You will report when you are in a position effectively to carry out the essential functions of Supreme Command, so that your assumption of command may be promulgated to all concerned.

18. SUPERIOR AUTHORITY. -

As Supreme Commander of the ABDA Area you will be directly responsible to the ABDA Governments through the agency defined in Annex 2.

Signed

(By Power furnishing
Supreme Commander)

Countersigned:

Other ABDA Representatives.

U. S. SECRET
BRITISH MOST SECRET

ANNEX 1

(TO ANNEX 3, JCCSs-6)

BOUNDARIES OF ABDA AREA

1. The ABDA Area is bounded as follows:

On the North: By the boundary between India and Burma, thence eastward along the Chinese frontier and coastline to the latitude of 30° North, thence along the parallel of 30° North to the meridian of 140° East.

Note: Indo-China and Thailand are not included in this area.

On the East: By the meridian of 140° East from 30° North, to the equator, thence east to longitude 141° East, thence South to the boundary of Dutch New Guinea on the South Coast, thence east along the Southern New Guinea Coast to the meridian of 143° East, then south down this meridian to the coast of Australia.

On the South: By the northern coast of Australia from the meridian of 143° East, westward to the meridian of 114° East, thence northwestward to latitude 15° South, longitude 92° East.

On the West: By the meridian of 92° East.

2. Forces assigned to the ABDA and adjacent areas are authorized to extend their operations into other areas as may be required.

U. S. SECRET
BRITISH MOST SECRET

ANNEX 2

(TO ANNEX 3, JCCSs-6)

December 30, 1941

HIGHER DIRECTION OF WAR IN THE ABDA AREA

1. On all important military matters, not within the jurisdiction of the Supreme Commander of the ABDA Area, the U. S. Chiefs of Staff and the representatives in Washington of the British Chiefs of Staff will constitute the agency for developing and submitting recommendations for decision by the President of the United States and by the British Prime Minister and Minister of Defense. Among the chief matters on which decisions will be required are:

    a. The provision of reinforcements.
    b. A major change in policy.
    c. Departure from the Supreme Commander's directive.

2. This agency will function as follows:

    a. Any proposal coming either from the Supreme Commander or from any of the ABDA governments will be transmitted to the Chiefs of Staff Committee both in Washington and in London.

    b. The Chiefs of Staff Committee in London will immediately telegraph to their representatives in Washington to say whether or not they will be telegraphing any opinions.

    c. On receipt of these opinions, the U. S. Chiefs of Staff and the representatives in Washington of the British Chiefs of Staff will develop and submit their recommendations to the President, and by telegraph to the Prime Minister and Minister of Defense. The Prime Minister will then inform the President whether he is in agreement with these recommendations.

3. Since London has the machinery for consulting the Dominion Governments, and since the Dutch Government is in London, the British Government will be responsible for obtaining their views and agreement, and for including these in the final telegram to Washington.

4. Agreement having been reached between the President and the Prime Minister and Minister of Defense, the orders to the Supreme Commander will be dispatched from Washington in the name of both of them.

U. S. SECRET
BRITISH MOST SECRET

ABC-4
JCCSs-7   December 31, 1941

THE CHIEFS OF STAFF CONFERENCE

FEDERAL RESERVE BUILDING

WASHINGTON, D. C.

2 P.M., DECEMBER 31, 1941

Present

British Officers

   Navy

      Admiral of the Fleet, Sir Dudley Pound, First Sea Lord and Chief of
                                                Naval Staff
      Admiral Sir Charles Little, Joint Staff Mission

   Army

      Field Marshal Sir John Dill
      Lieut. General Sir Colville Wemyss, Joint Staff Mission

   Air Force

      Air Marshal A. T. Harris, Joint Staff Mission.

United States Officers

   Navy

      Admiral H. R. Stark, Chief of Naval Operations
      Admiral E. J. King, Commander-in-Chief, U. S. Fleet
               (Present for only part of the Conference)
      Rear Admiral W. R. Sexton, President, General Board
      Rear Admiral J. H. Towers, Chief, Bureau of Aeronautics
      Rear Admiral R. K. Turner, Director, War Plans Division
      Commander R. E. Libby, Aide to Commander-in-Chief, U. S. Fleet
      Major General Thomas Holcomb, Commandant, U. S. M. C.

- 1 -

U. S. SECRET
BRITISH MOST SECRET

Army

    General George C. Marshall, Commanding General of the Field Forces and Chief of Staff
    Lieut. General H. H. Arnold, Chief of the Army Air Forces and Deputy Chief of Staff
    Brigadier General L. T. Gerow, Chief of War Plans Division
    Brigadier General D. D. Eisenhower, General Staff Corps.

Joint Secretaries

    Colonel E. I. C. Jacob
    Captain J. L. McCrea, Aide to Chief of Naval Operations
    Lieut. Colonel P. M. Robinett, G-2, GHQ, U.S.A.
    Major W. T. Sexton, Assistant Secretary, W.D.G.S.

1.   WITHDRAWAL OF UNITED STATES MARINES FROM ICELAND. -

ADMIRAL STARK said that he was very anxious to withdraw the 4,500 U. S. Marines from Iceland as soon as possible, as they were urgently needed for other tasks. He hoped that this could be arranged even at the risk of delay in the relief of British troops.

MARSHAL DILL agreed as to the importance of withdrawing the Marines. He suggested that the local Commanders might be instructed to draw up the best possible plan for arranging this withdrawal as early as possible. He would telegraph to England to give the necessary instructions.

ADMIRAL STARK said that the details of what was required could be furnished by Brigadier General Gerow.

It was agreed that the withdrawal of the 4,500 U. S. Marines now serving in Iceland should be arranged as soon as possible and SIR JOHN DILL undertook to telegraph the necessary instructions to England on receipt of the details of what was required from Brigadier General Gerow.

2.   AMERICAN-BRITISH STRATEGY. -

THE CONFERENCE considered a revised version, prepared by the U. S. Chiefs of Staff, of the Memorandum on American-British Strategy. (WW-1. U.S Revised). The various amendments proposed by the U. S. Chiefs of Staff were considered, and with a few exceptions were agreed to. It was also decided that the lists of sea and air bases contained in Paragraph 12 should be omitted. It was further agreed that the paper should be circulated only to the United States and British Chiefs of Staff and their immediate subordinates, and that a note should be inserted in the paper to this effect.

U. S. SECRET
BRITISH MOST SECRET

AIR MARSHAL HARRIS said he would like to check with General Arnold the list of Air Routes which had been inserted.

Subject to a final check by Air Marshal Harris with General Arnold of the Air Routes paragraph, the U. S. and British Chiefs of Staff approved the memorandum (See Annex No. 1), American-British Strategy, WW-1 (Final)), on American-British Strategy as amended in the discussion, and agreed that it should be submitted to the President and the Prime Minister.

3. SUPPORTING MEASURES FOR THE SOUTHWEST PACIFIC. -

THE CONFERENCE considered a report (U.S. ABC-4/3, British WW (J.P.C.)3), by the Joint Planning Committee on supporting measures for the Southwest Pacific.

ADMIRAL POUND said that as there would be an interval before General Wavell could take up his command, he thought it would be desirable to dispatch a telegram to the U. S. and British Commanders-in-Chief in the Far East to inform them of the general policy which had been agreed upon by the Chiefs of Staff. He handed across copies of a telegram which he had drafted for this purpose. The draft telegram was considered and a number of amendments were agreed upon.

Later in the meeting, after Admiral King had entered, further consideration was given to the telegram, and some additional amendments made. A few minor amendments to the report were also accepted by the Joint Planning Committee.

It was agreed:

a. That the telegram, as amended in the discussion, should be dispatched forthwith to United States and British Commanders in the Far East.

b. That the report by the Joint Planning Committee, subject to the incorporation of the minor amendments agreed to in the discussion, should be approved.

The report and the telegram in their final form were subsequently circulated as U.S. ABC-4/3, British WW-4 (See Annex 2.)

4. NORTHWEST AFRICA PROJECT. -

ADMIRAL STARK said that the United States Chiefs of Staff were not ready to discuss the report by the Joint Planning Committee on this subject, (U.S. ABC-4/2, British WW (J.P.C.)2).

U. S. SECRET
BRITISH MOST SECRET

ADMIRAL POUND said that certain officers bringing full information on reinforcements and shipping programs were expected to arrive from the United Kingdom on the following day. He thought that the Joint Planning Committee should then be in a position to examine the three main problems which were confronting us in the near future: namely,

    a. Northwest Africa Project.
    b. Relief of British Garrisons in Northern Ireland and Iceland.
    c. Reinforcements for the Far East and consequent replacements in the Middle East.

He thought that there were two cases which should be considered. First, one should assume that reinforcements to the Far East must be given priority; to what extent then must the gaps in the Middle East be filled, and could the Northwest Africa project be carried out? Alternatively, supposing the Northwest Africa project had to be carried out by invitation in the immediate future, what would happen to the rest of the program?

ADMIRAL STARK said that with the Naval resources at present available, it did not appear possible to undertake anything which involved opening up a new convoy route.

REAR ADMIRAL TURNER said that the Joint Planning Committee felt the Northwest Africa project should be considered under more realistic hypotheses. Guidance from the Chiefs of Staff was required on this point. It should be realized that entry into French North Africa was only possible through Casablanca, which was a good but small port. The maximum rate at which forces could be disembarked was that given in the report, and this would be inadequate if opposition was likely to be met.

ADMIRAL STARK thought that the Joint Planning Committee should consider what could be done in French North Africa if the situation was different from that assumed in the present report.

After further discussion, it was agreed that the Joint Planning Committee should be instructed to examine the questions in view of the discussion which had been raised.

GENERAL MARSHALL asked -- on the assumption that it would be impossible to enter Morocco under resistance and the Germans moved through Spain -- what would be the next move?

ADMIRAL POUND replied, the occupation of the Canaries.

(At this point Admiral King entered the meeting).

U.S. SECRET
BRITISH MOST SECRET

5. RELIEF OF THE BRITISH GARRISON IN NORTHERN IRELAND. -

ADMIRAL KING said that it had been decided that for the present, U. S. forces destined for the relief of the British garrison in Northern Ireland should be transported in the S. S. GEORGE WASHINGTON, which would shortly be fit for service, this vessel being used on a continuous shuttle service to and from Northern Ireland. In a few weeks' time, when the general trend in the Atlantic theatre could be judged, a decision could be taken as to whether the transport of these troops should be accelerated or not.

THE CONFERENCE took note of this statement.

6. DRAFT DIRECTIVE TO THE SUPREME COMMANDER IN THE ABDA AREA. -

The Conference gave further consideration to this directive (U S. ABC-4/5, British WW (J.P.C.)5). One minor verbal alteration was agreed to and it was also decided to bring the statement of the general strategic policy into line with that telegraphed out to Commanders-in-Chief in the Far East by defining the Malay Barrier. (See Annex 2.)

ADMIRAL KING said that he had reason to believe that the directive would meet with the approval of the President, and this also applied to the statement on the higher direction of war in the ABDA Area contained in U.S. ABC-4/5, British WW-3 (Final), (See Annex 3.) He had also received a request that the U. S. and British Chiefs of Staff should draft for consideration the public announcement setting up the unified command in the ABDA Area. He thought this should be completed on Friday.

THE U. S. AND BRITISH CHIEFS OF STAFF gave final approval to the draft directive to the Supreme Commander of the ABDA Area as amended in the discussion (U.S. ABC-4/5, British WW-3 (Final), (See Annex 3), and took note of Admiral King's statement.

7. PROPOSED TASKS FOR THE JOINT PLANNING COMMITTEE. -

The Conference considered the statement of tasks proposed for the Joint Planning Committee in U. S. Serial ABC-4/4, British WW (J.P.C.) 4, (See Annex 4.) At the suggestion of Admiral Stark, it was decided that the following note should be added to the end of the paper:

"Consideration of the Southwest Pacific theatre, including the matter of unity of command therein, was treated as a first priority, and a decision reached prior to the acceptance of the foregoing document."

The U. S. and British Chiefs of Staff accepted the statement (Annex 4, U.S. ABC-4/4, British WW (J.P.C.)4), of the proposed tasks

U. S. SECRET
BRITISH MOST SECRET

for the Joint Planning Committee, subject to the insertion of the note recorded above.

    8.   NAVAL DISPOSITIONS. -

SIR DUDLEY POUND suggested that one of the matters which might be discussed was the size of the Naval Forces available in the ABDA Area, and whether they were sufficient for the tasks they would encounter.

There was some discussion on this point in the course of which ADMIRAL KING pointed out that such a study would necessitate examination of the Naval resources in other theatres.

It was stated that the Naval staffs were already at work on this, and it was finally agreed that this point should continue to be dealt with by them in direct consultation.

The Conference adjourned at 5:15 P.M.

ENCLOSURES
    Annex 1 - American British Strategy. U.S.-ABC 4/CS1 British WW-1.
    Annex 2 - Supporting Measures for the Southwest Pacific, U.S.-ABC-4/3 British WW-4, with Telegram and 3 Annexes.
    Annex 3 - Directive To Supreme Commander in ABDA Area, U.S.-ABC-4/5 British WW-3, with 2 Annexes.
    Annex 4 - Proposed Tasks for the Joint Planning Committee, U.S. ABC-4/4 British WW (JPC)4.

U. S. SECRET
BRITISH MOST SECRET

U.S. ABC-4/CS1
BRITISH WW-1 (FINAL)   December 31, 1941

ANNEX 1
to
JCCSs-7

UNITED STATES - BRITISH

CHIEFS OF STAFF

APPROVED

MEMORANDUM BY THE U. S. AND BRITISH CHIEFS
OF STAFF

AMERICAN - BRITISH

GRAND STRATEGY

U. S. SECRET
BRITISH MOST SECRET

U.S. SERIAL ABC-4/CS-1
BRITISH SERIAL W.W.-1 (FINAL)

TO BE KEPT UNDER LOCK AND KEY

It is requested that special
care may be taken to ensure the
secrecy of this document.

WASHINGTON WAR CONFERENCE

AMERICAN-BRITISH STRATEGY

MEMORANDUM BY THE UNITED STATES AND BRITISH CHIEFS OF STAFF

NOTE: The circulation of this paper should be restricted to the United States and British Chiefs of Staff and their immediate subordinates.

I. GRAND STRATEGY

1. At the A-B* Staff conversations in February, 1941, it was agreed that Germany was the predominant member of the Axis Powers, and consequently the Atlantic and European area was considered to be the decisive theatre.

2. Much has happened since February last, but notwithstanding the entry of Japan into the War, our view remains that Germany is still the prime enemy and her defeat is the key to victory. Once Germany is defeated, the collapse of Italy and the defeat of Japan must follow.

3. In our considered opinion, therefore, it should be a cardinal principle of A-B strategy that only the minimum of force necessary for the safeguarding of vital interests in other theatres should be diverted from operations against Germany.

II. ESSENTIAL FEATURES OF OUR STRATEGY

4. The essential features of the above grand strategy are as follows. Each will be examined in greater detail later in this paper.

   a. The realization of the victory programme of armaments, which first and foremost requires the security of the main areas of war industry.

Note:-
 * For brevity the abbreviated
   A-B is used to denote
   American-British

U. S. SECRET
BRITISH MOST SECRET

    b. The maintenance of essential communications.

    c. Closing and tightening the ring around Germany.

    d. Wearing down and undermining German resistance by air bombardment, blockade, subversive activities and propaganda.

    e. The continuous development of offensive action against Germany.

    f. Maintaining only such positions in the Eastern theatre as will safeguard vital interests (see paragraph 18) and denying to Japan access to raw materials vital to her continuous war effort while we are concentrating on the defeat of Germany.

    III. STEPS TO BE TAKEN IN 1942 TO PUT INTO EFFECT THE

ABOVE GENERAL POLICY.

THE SECURITY OF AREAS OF WAR PRODUCTION

5. In so far as these are likely to be attacked, the main areas of war industry are situated in:—

    a. The United Kingdom.

    b. Continental United States, particularly the West Coast.

    c. Russia.

6. THE UNITED KINGDOM. - To safeguard the United Kingdom it will be necessary to maintain at all times the minimum forces required to defeat invasion.

7. THE UNITED STATES. - The main centers of production on or near the West Coast of United States must be protected from Japanese sea-borne attack. This will be facilitated by holding Hawaii and Alaska. We consider that a Japanese invasion of the United States on a large scale is highly improbable, whether Hawaii or Alaska is held or not.

8. The probable scale of attack and the general nature of the forces required for the defense of the United States are matters for the United States Chiefs of Staff to assess.

9. RUSSIA. - It will be essential to afford the Russians assistance to enable them to maintain their hold on Leningrad, Moscow, and the oilfields of the Caucasus, and to continue their war effort.

U. S. SECRET
BRITISH MOST SECRET

MAINTENANCE OF COMMUNICATIONS

10. THE MAIN SEA ROUTES WHICH MUST BE SECURED ARE:-

   a. From the United States to the United Kingdom.

   b. From the United States and the United Kingdom to North Russia.

   c. The various routes from the United Kingdom and the United States to Freetown, South America, and the Cape.

   d. The routes in the Indian Ocean to the Red Sea and Persian Gulf, to India and Burma, to the East Indies, and to Australasia.

   e. The route through the Panama Canal, and the United States coastal traffic.

   f. The Pacific routes from the United States and the Panama Canal to Alaska, Hawaii, Australia, and the Far East.

   In addition to the above routes, we shall do everything possible to open up and secure the Mediterranean route.

11. THE MAIN AIR ROUTES WHICH MUST BE SECURED ARE:-

   a. From the United States to South America, Ascension, Freetown, Takoradi, and Cairo.

   b. From the United Kingdom to Gibraltar, Malta and Cairo.

   c. From Cairo to Karachi, Calcutta, China, Malaya, Philippines, Australasia.

   d. From the United States to Australia via Hawaii, Christmas Island, Canton, Palmyra, Samoa, Fiji, New Caledonia.

   e. The routes from Australia to the Philippines and Malaya via the Netherlands East Indies.

   f. From the United States to the United Kingdom via Newfoundland, Canada, Greenland, and Iceland.

   g. From the United States to the United Kingdom via the Azores.

   h. From the United States to Vladivostok, via Alaska.

U. S. SECRET
BRITISH MOST SECRET

    12.   THE SECURITY OF THESE ROUTES INVOLVES:-

        a. Well-balanced A - B naval and air dispositions.

        b. Holding and capturing essential sea and air bases.

CLOSING AND TIGHTENING THE RING AROUND GERMANY

    13.   This ring may be defined as a line running roughly as follows: ARCHANGEL - BLACK SEA - ANATOLIA - THE NORTHERN SEABOARD OF THE MEDITERRANEAN - THE WESTERN SEABOARD OF EUROPE.

    The main object will be to strengthen this ring, and close the gaps in it, by sustaining the Russian front, by arming and supporting Turkey, by increasing our strength in the Middle East, and by gaining possession of the whole North African coast.

    14.   If this ring can be closed, the blockade of Germany and Italy will be complete, and German eruptions, e.g. towards the Persian Gulf, or to the Atlantic seaboard of Africa, will be prevented. Furthermore, the seizing of the North African coast may open the Mediterranean to convoys, thus enormously shortening the route to the Middle East and saving considerable tonnage now employed in the long haul around the Cape.

THE UNDERMINING AND WEARING DOWN OF THE GERMAN RESISTANCE

    15.   In 1942 the main methods of wearing down Germany's resistance will be:-

        a. Ever-increasing air bombardment by British and American Forces.

        b. Assistance to Russia's offensive by all available means.

        c. The blockade.

        d. The maintenance of the spirit of revolt in the occupied countries, and the organization of subversive movements.

DEVELOPMENT OF LAND OFFENSIVES ON THE CONTINENT

    16.   It does not seem likely that in 1942 any large scale land offensive against Germany except on the Russian front will be possible. We must, however, be ready to take advantage of any opening that may result from the wearing down process referred to in paragraph 15 to conduct limited land offensives.

U. S. SECRET
BRITISH MOST SECRET

17. In 1943 the way may be clear for a return to the Continent, across the Mediterranean, from Turkey into the Balkans, or by landings in Western Europe. Such operations will be the prelude to the final assault on Germany itself, and the scope of the victory program should be such as to provide means by which they can be carried out.

THE SAFEGUARDING OF VITAL INTERESTS IN THE EASTERN THEATRE

18. The security of Australia, New Zealand, and India must be maintained, and the Chinese war effort supported. Secondly, points of vantage from which an offensive against Japan can eventually be developed must be secured. Our immediate object must therefore be to hold:-

    a. Hawaii and Alaska.

    b. Singapore, the East Indies Barrier, and the Philippines.

    c. Rangoon and the route to China.

    d. The Maritime Provinces of Siberia.

The minimum forces required to hold the above will have to be a matter of mutual discussion.

U. S. SECRET
BRITISH MOST SECRET

U.S. ABC-4/3   ANNEX 2   December 31, 1941
BRITISH WW-4   to
                            JCCSs-7

REPORT

By

UNITED STATES - BRITISH

CHIEFS OF STAFF

SUPPORTING MEASURES FOR THE SOUTHWEST PACIFIC

(THE FAR EAST AREA AND ADJACENT REGIONS)

UNTIL ESTABLISHMENT OF UNIFIED COMMAND.

U. S. SECRET
BRITISH MOST SECRET

U.S. ABC-4/3   December 31, 1941
BRITISH WW(J.P.C.)3

       The United States and British Chiefs of Staff approved the Joint Planning Committee report of December 29, 1941, on "Supporting Measures for the Southwest Pacific" as appropriate action to be taken in the interim prior to the establishment of the unified command of the forces in that region.

       The United States and British Chiefs of Staff agreed to send immediately to the United States and British Commanders-in-Chief in the Far East Area the following telegram:

       "The general strategic policy for operations in the Far Eastern theatre which has been agreed upon by the United States and British Chiefs of Staff is as follows:-

       a. To hold the Malay Barrier, defined as the line Malay Peninsula, Sumatra, Java, and North Australia, as the basic defensive position in that theatre and to operate sea, land, and air forces in as great depth as possible forward of the Barrier in order to oppose the Japanese southward advance.

       b. To hold Burma and Australia as essential supporting positions for the theatre, and Burma as essential to the support of China, and to the defense of India.

       c. To reestablish communications through the Dutch East Indies with Luzon and to support the Philippines' Garrison.

       d. To maintain essential communications within the theatre.

       In disposing of the reinforcements arriving in that theatre, you should be guided by the above policy and consider the needs of the theatre as a whole. To this end, close co-operation among the British, Dutch and United States Commanders is essential, and you should continue to concert measures accordingly.

       The British Commander-in-Chief, Far East, will inform the Dutch and request their cooperation."

TELEGRAM

U. S. SECRET
BRITISH MOST SECRET

U.S. SERIAL ABC-4/3　　　　　　　　　　　　　　　　　　December 28, 1941
BRITISH SERIAL WW(J.P.C.) 3.

JOINT PLANNING COMMITTEE REPORT

TO

CHIEFS OF STAFF

SUPPORTING MEASURES FOR THE SOUTHWEST PACIFIC

(THE FAR EAST AREA AND ADJACENT REGIONS)

DIRECTIVE

1. CHIEFS OF STAFF DIRECTIVE TO THE JOINT PLANNING COMMITTEE.

Until such time as the wider problem of the unified control of all available forces in the Southwest Pacific Area is solved, the aim must be to reinforce the Philippine Islands, Malaya, and the Netherlands East Indies, to the maximum extent, and to make the best possible arrangements for ensuring the safe arrival and the most effective intervention of these reinforcements.

Having regard to the existing situation in the Far East and the Southwest Pacific, the Joint Planning Committee is asked to make recommendations as to the disposition of the reinforcements, particularly air forces, expected to be available in the Southwest Pacific Area on:-

    a. 15th January, 1942.

    b. 1st February, 1942.

on the following alternative assumptions:-

    (1) The Philippines and Singapore both hold.

    (2) Singapore and the Netherlands East Indies hold, but the Philippines do not.

    (3) Neither Singapore nor the Philippines holds.

CONCEPT OF OPERATIONS

2. Our basic strategic concept is to maintain initially the strategic defensive in the Southwest Pacific Theatre. The present strength

U. S. SECRET
BRITISH MOST SECRET

of forces in that area is insufficient to maintain that defensive position.

After providing immediate reinforcements for defense, and as additional forces become available, it will become possible to undertake offensive operations and ultimately to conduct an all-out offensive against Japan. Accordingly, although our operations in the near future must be primarily for defense, they should be so conducted as to further our preparations for a future offensive.

3. The general strategic policy should therefore be:-

a. To hold the Malay Barrier, defined as the line Malay Peninsula, Sumatra, Java, North Australia, as the basic defensive position of the Far East Area, and to operate air and sea forces in as great depth as possible forward of the Barrier in order to oppose the Japanese southward advance.

b. To hold Burma and Australia as essential supporting positions for the Far East Area, and Burma as essential to the support of China and to the defense of India.

c. To reestablish communications with Luzon and to support the Philippines' Garrison.

d. To maintain communications to Burma and Australia, and to and within the Far East Area.

e. To obtain in the Far East Area and Australasia all possible supplies to relieve shipping requirements.

FORCES AND REINFORCEMENTS

4. The estimated strength of forces initially in the Area, and the reinforcements ordered or planned to be sent are shown in the attached tables (Annexes I, II, and III). Future reinforcements should be planned in accordance with approved strategic policy, having due regard to the essential requirements of other theatres.

RECOMMENDATIONS

5. It is recommended that, until such time as the wider problem of the unified control of all available forces in the Southwest Pacific Area is solved:-

U. S. SECRET
BRITISH MOST SECRET

    a. Under the assumption that the Philippines and Singapore both hold, the total reinforcements available up to 1st February, 1942, as shown on the attached table, should go forward as now arranged, subject to the direction of the commander to whom they are assigned.

    b. Under the assumption that Singapore and the Netherlands East Indies hold, but the Philippines do not, the total United States reinforcements available up to 1st February, 1942, should be employed in furtherance of the defenses of key points on the Malay Barrier, and for protection of the vital lines of communication from the east. In the absence of unity of command, detailed dispositions of these reinforcements must be left to the senior United States Army commander, in collaboration with the senior British, Dutch, and Australian commanders. Under this assumption the planned disposition of British reinforcements remains unchanged.

    c. Under the assumption that neither Singapore nor the Philippines holds, the total reinforcements available up to 1st February, 1942, be used for the defense of the remainder of the Malay Barrier, Burma, and Australia, United States reinforcements being used to the eastward, and British reinforcements to the westward.

NOTE:- The subject of reinforcements for New Zealand and Fiji is being considered separately.

U. S. SECRET
BRITISH MOST SECRET

FAR EAST FORCES AND REINFORCEMENTS THEREFOR

UNITED STATES

FORCES NOW IN THE FAR EAST	DUE IN FAR EAST BY JANUARY 15, 1942	DUE IN FAR EAST BETWEEN JAN. 15 AND FEBRUARY 1	TENTATIVELY PLANNED OR UNDER ORDER FOR FAR EAST
(a) <u>Naval</u>	(a) <u>Naval</u>	(a) <u>Naval</u>	(a) <u>Naval</u>
2 Cruisers 18 Destroyers (3 damaged) 27 Submarines (less losses) 7 Patrol Bombers	12 Patrol Bombers	None	None
(b) <u>Army</u>	(b) <u>Army</u>	(b) <u>Army</u>	(b) <u>Army</u>
<u>Philippines</u> (Luzon) 40,000 as of December 22, 1941. <u>Australia</u> 2 Regts Field Artillery Service Troops	Small Arms Ammunition Artillery Ammunition AA Ammunition Gasoline	None	Supplies & Gasoline
(c) <u>Air</u>	(c) <u>Air</u>	(c) <u>Air</u>	(c) <u>Air</u>
<u>Philippines (Dec. 25)</u> Few Pursuit planes for reconnaissance <u>Australia</u> 18 Pursuit planes 52 Dive bombers 11 Heavy Bombers	55 Pursuit 23 Heavy Bombers	67 Pursuit 57 Heavy Bombers	To make total of: 4 Gps. Pursuit (320) 2 Gps. Heavy Bombers (70) 2 Gps. Medium Bombers (114) 1 Gp. Light Bombers (57) (plus certain reserves)

ANNEX I

U. S. SECRET
BRITISH MOST SECRET

FAR EAST FORCES AND REINFORCEMENTS THEREFOR

BRITISH COMMONWEALTH

FORCES IN THE FAR EAST ON DECEMBER 7, 1941	DUE IN FAR EAST BY JANUARY 15, 1942	DUE IN FAR EAST BETWEEN JANUARY 15 AND FEBRUARY 1	TENTATIVELY PLANNED OR UNDER ORDER FOR FAR EAST
(a) <u>Naval</u> 2 Cruisers 8 Destroyers	(a) <u>Naval</u> 5 Additional Escort Vessels	(a) <u>Naval</u> 2 Submarines	(a) <u>Naval</u> None
(b) <u>Army</u> 9 and 11 Ind. Divs.) 8 Aus. Div.) Malaya (less one Bde.) One Div. (Burma) 2 Inf. Bdes. (Singapore)	(b) <u>Army (to Malaya)</u> One Bde. Gp. 17 Ind. Div. One Bde. Gp. 18 Div. One AA Regt. (light) One AA Regt. (heavy) One Antitank Regt.	(b) <u>Army (to Malaya)</u> One Bde. Gp. 17 Ind. Div. One Bde. Gp. 18 Div. Drafts for 9 and 11 Ind. Divs. One Sq. Light Tanks.	(b) <u>Army (Malaya)</u> Two AA Regts. (light) One AA Regt. (heavy) One Bde. Gp. 14 Ind. Div. 18 Div. (less two Bde. Gps). <u>To Burma</u> 14 Ind. Div. (less one Bde. Gp.) One Bde. Gp. 17th Ind. Div. 5th or 34th Ind. Div.
(c) <u>Air</u> <u>Malaya</u> 2 Bomber Sqns. 2 Bomber Recce Sqns. 6 Fighter Sqns. 2 T.B. Sqns 1 G.R. Flying Boat Sqn.	(c) <u>Air</u> <u>Malaya</u> 4 PBY's 1 Fighter Sq. (51 Hurricanes) 1 Bomber Sq. (Blenheims) 1 Bomber Recce (Hudsons)	(c) <u>Air</u> <u>Malaya</u> 2 Fighter Sqns. (48 Hurricanes)	(c) <u>Air</u> Plans not complete
<u>Burma</u> 1 Bomber Sqn. 1 Fighter Sqn.	<u>Burma</u> None	<u>Burma</u> 1 Fighter Sqn. (Hurricanes)	

ANNEX II

U. S. SECRET
BRITISH MOST SECRET

AUSTRALIA

Forces now in the Far East

(a) Naval

    2 Heavy Cruisers
    2 Light Cruisers
    4 Destroyers

(b) Army

    1 Brig. Gp. of 8th
       Australian Div.
    5 Divisions (Infantry)
    2 Divisions (Cavalry)
    1 Division (Armored)
       (Not as yet equipped)

(c) Air

    160 First line planes
    300 - 400 Training planes
  15,000 Air officers and men
  40,000 In Training

DUTCH

Forces now in the Far East

(a) Naval

    4 Cruisers
    7 Destroyers
  15 Submarines
  2 - 3 Submarines (Expected)
               (Later)

(b) Army

    3 Div's Java
    7 Bn's Sumatra
    4 Bn's Borneo
    1 Bn Celebes
    1 Bn Timor
    1 Bn Moluccas

(c) Air

    6 Bomber Sqns.
    4 Fighter Sqns.
  108 Navy Aircraft
  40 Patrol Planes

ANNEX III

U. S. SECRET
BRITISH MOST SECRET

U.S. ABC-4/5
BRITISH WW-3 (FINAL)

December 31, 1941

ANNEX 3
to
JCCSs-7

REPORT

By

UNITED STATES - BRITISH

CHIEFS OF STAFF

DRAFT DIRECTIVE TO THE SUPREME

COMMANDER IN THE ABDA AREA

NOTE:

Annex 2 To This Document
Was Amended Later.
(See Annex 1 To JCCSs-8)

U. S. SECRET
BRITISH MOST SECRET

U. S. SERIAL ABC-4/5
BRITISH SERIAL WW-3 (FINAL)　　　　　　　　　　　　　December 31, 1941

DRAFT DIRECTIVE TO THE

SUPREME COMMANDER

BY AGREEMENT AMONG THE GOVERNMENTS OF AUSTRALIA, THE NETHERLANDS,
THE UNITED KINGDOM, AND THE UNITED STATES, HEREINAFTER
REFERRED TO AS THE ABDA GOVERNMENTS:

1. AREA. -

A strategic area has been constituted, to comprise initially all land and sea areas included in the general region Burma - Malaya - Netherlands East Indies and the Philippines; more precisely defined in Annex 1. This area will be known as the ABDA Area.

2. FORCES. -

You have been designated as the Supreme Commander of the ABDA Area and of all armed forces, afloat, ashore, and in the air, of the ABDA Governments, which are:

    a. Stationed in the Area;

    b. Located in Australian territory when such forces have been allotted by the respective governments for services in or in support of the ABDA Area.

You are not authorized to transfer from the territory of any of the ABDA Governments land forces of that government without the consent of the local commander or his government.

3. The Deputy Supreme Commander and, if required, a commander of the combined naval forces and a commander of the combined air forces will be jointly designated by the ABDA Governments.

4. No government will materially reduce its armed forces assigned to your Area nor any commitments made by it for reinforcing its forces in your Area except after giving to the other governments, and to you, timely information pertaining thereto.

5. STRATEGIC CONCEPT AND POLICY. -

The basic strategic concept of the ABDA Governments for the conduct

U. S. SECRET
BRITISH MOST SECRET

of the war in your Area is to maintain initially the strategic defensive. The ABDA Governments intend to provide immediate reinforcements for defense. As additional forces become available, it will become possible to take the offensive and ultimately to conduct an all-out offensive against Japan. The first essential is to gain general air superiority at the earliest possible moment, through the employment of concentrated air power. The piecemeal employment of air forces should be minimized. Although your operations in the near future must be primarily for defense, they should be so conducted as to further preparations for that offensive.

6. The general strategic policy will therefore be: -

   <u>a</u>. To hold the Malay Barrier, defined as the line Malay Peninsula, Sumatra, Java, North Australia, as the basic defensive position of the ABDA Area, and to operate sea, land, and air forces in as great depth as possible forward of the Barrier in order to oppose the Japanese southward advance.

   <u>b</u>. To hold Burma and Australia as essential supporting positions for the Area, and Burma as essential to the support of China, and to the defense of India.

   <u>c</u>. To re-establish communications through the Dutch East Indies with Luzon and to support the Philippines' Garrison.

   <u>d</u>. To maintain essential communications within the Area.

7. DUTIES, RESPONSIBILITIES, AND AUTHORITY OF THE SUPREME COMMANDER. -

   You will coordinate in the ABDA Area the strategic operations of all armed forces of the ABDA Governments; assign them strategic missions and objectives; where desirable, arrange for the formation of task forces, whether national or international, for the execution of specific operations; and appoint any officer, irrespective of seniority or nationality, to command such task forces.

8. While you will have no responsibilities in respect of the internal administration of the respective forces under your command, you are authorized to direct and coordinate the creation and development of administrative facilities and the broad allocation of war materials.

9. You will dispose reinforcements which from time to time may be dispatched to the Area by the ABDA Governments.

10. You are authorized to require from the Commanders of the armed forces under your command such reports as you deem necessary in the discharge of your responsibilities as Supreme Commander.

U. S. SECRET
BRITISH MOST SECRET

11. You are authorized to control the issue of all communiques concerning the forces under your command.

12. Through the channels specified in Paragraph 18, you may submit recommendations to the ABDA Governments on any matters pertaining to the furtherance of your mission.

13. LIMITATIONS. -

Your authority and control with respect to the various portions of the ABDA Area and to the forces assigned thereto will normally be exercised through the commanders duly designated by their respective governments. Interference is to be avoided in the administrative processes of the armed forces of any of the ABDA Governments, including free communication between them and their respective governments. No alteration or revision is to be made in the basic tactical organization of such forces, and each national component of a task force will normally operate under its own commander and will not be subdivided into small units for attachment to the other national components of the task force. In general, your instructions and orders will be limited to those necessary for effective coordination of forces in the execution of your mission.

14. RELATIONS WITH ABDA GOVERNMENTS. -

The ABDA Governments will jointly and severally support you in the execution of the duties and responsibilities as herein defined, and in the exercise of the authority herein delegated and limited. Commanders of all sea, land, and air forces within your Area will be immediately informed by their respective governments that, from a date to be notified, all orders and instructions issued by you in conformity with the provisions of this directive will be considered by such commanders as emanating from their respective governments.

15. If any of your immediate subordinates, after making due representation to you, still considers that obedience to your orders would jeopardize the national interests of his country to an extent unjustified by the general situation in the ABDA Area, he has the right, subject to your being immediately notified of such intention, to appeal direct to his own government before carrying out the orders. Such appeals will be made by the most expeditious method, and a copy of the appeal will be communicated simultaneously to you.

16. STAFF AND ASSUMPTION OF COMMAND. -

Your staff will include officers of each of the ABDA powers. You are empowered to communicate immediately with the national commanders in the

U. S. SECRET
BRITISH MOST SECRET

Area with a view to obtaining staff officers essential to your earliest possible assumption of command. Your additional staff requirements will be communicated as soon as possible to the ABDA Governments through channels of communication described in Paragraph 18.

17. You will report when you are in a position effectively to carry out the essential functions of Supreme Command, so that your assumption of command may be promulgated to all concerned.

18. SUPERIOR AUTHORITY. -

As Supreme Commander of the ABDA Area, you will be directly responsible to the ABDA Governments through the agency defined in Annex 2.

                                              Signed

                                              (By Power furnishing
                                                Supreme Commander)

Countersigned:

    Other ABDA Representatives.

U. S. SECRET
BRITISH MOST SECRET

ANNEX 1

BOUNDARIES OF ABDA AREA

1. The ABDA Area is bounded as follows:

   On the North: By the boundary between India and Burma, thence eastward along the Chinese frontier and coastline to the latitude of 30° North, thence along the parallel of 30° North to the meridian of 140° East.

   Note: Indo-China and Thailand are not included in this area.

   On the East: By the meridian of 140° East from 30° North, to the equator, thence east to longitude 141° East, thence south to the boundary of Dutch New Guinea on the south coast, thence east along the southern New Guinea Coast to the meridian of 143° East, then south down this meridian to the coast of Australia.

   On the South: By the northern coast of Australia from the meridian of 143° East, westward to the meridian of 114° East, thence northwestward to latitude 15° South, longitude 92° East.

   On the West: By the meridian of 92° East.

2. Forces assigned to the ABDA and adjacent areas are authorized to extend their operations into other areas as may be required.

U. S. SECRET
BRITISH MOST SECRET
December 31, 1941

ANNEX 2

HIGHER DIRECTION OF WAR IN THE ABDA AREA

1. On all important military matters, not within the jurisdiction of the Supreme Commander of the ABDA Area, the U. S. Chiefs of Staff and the representatives in Washington of the British Chiefs of Staff will constitute the agency for developing and submitting recommendations for decision by the President of the United States and by the British Prime Minister and Minister of Defence. Among the chief matters on which decisions will be required are:

    a. The provision of reinforcements.
    b. A major change in policy.
    c. Departure from the Supreme Commander's directive.

2. This agency will function as follows:

    a. Any proposal coming either from the Supreme Commander or from any of the ABDA governments will be transmitted to the Chiefs of Staff Committee both in Washington and in London.

    b. The Chiefs of Staff Committee in London will immediately telegraph to their representatives in Washington to say whether or not they will be telegraphing any opinions

    c. On receipt of these opinions, the U. S. Chiefs of Staff and the representatives in Washington of the British Chiefs of Staff will develop and submit their recommendations to the President, and by telegraph to the Prime Minister and Minister of Defence The Prime Minister will then inform the President whether he is in agreement with these recommendations.

3. Since London has the machinery for consulting the Dominion Governments, and since the Dutch Government is in London, the British Government will be responsible for obtaining their views and agreement, and for including these in the final telegram to Washington

4. Agreement having been reached between the President and the Prime Minister and Minister of Defence, the orders to the Supreme Commander will be dispatched from Washington in the name of both of them.

U. S. SECRET
BRITISH MOST SECRET

U. S. SERIAL ABC-4/4 (FINAL)　　　　　　　　　　　　　　　December 31, 1941
BRITISH SERIAL WW(J.P.C.)4

ANNEX 4
to
JCCSs-7

UNITED STATES - BRITISH

CHIEFS OF STAFF

APPROVED

PROPOSED TASKS FOR THE JOINT PLANNING

COMMITTEE

U. S. SECRET
BRITISH MOST SECRET

U.S. SERIAL ABC-4/4 (FINAL)
BRITISH SERIAL WW(J.P.C.)4

December 31, 1941

PROPOSED TASKS FOR THE JOINT PLANNING COMMITTEE

1. A study of the relative importance and interrelation of the various military projects and movements which affect the Atlantic theatre and which may be required to give effect to the agreed Grand Strategy during the first part of 1942.

   This report will include consideration of the following:

   a. MOVEMENTS

   (1) Relief of Iceland.

   (2) Movement of three Divisions and one Armored Division from the United States to Northern Ireland.

   (3) Movement of United States air forces to the United Kingdom.

   (4) Relief of British in Aruba and Curacao.

   b. PROJECTS

   (1) Joint United States-British occupation of French North Africa.

   (2) United States occupation of:

   (a) French West Africa and Cape Verde Islands.

   (b) Northeast Brazil.

   (3) British occupation of:

   (a) The Azores.

   (b) The Canaries and Madeira.

   (c) Diego Suarez.

2. Coordination of the Victory Programs of the United States and the British Commonwealth and adjustment of their broad outlines in accordance with strategic considerations and production possibilities.

U. S. SECRET
BRITISH MOST SECRET

3. A consideration of any steps that should be taken in the light of experience up to date to implement, improve, or extend the system of collaboration between the United States-British Staffs as laid down in ABC-1; the need for allocating joint resources on a strategic basis to be taken into account.

> NOTE: Consideration of the Southwest Pacific Theatre, including the matter of unity of command therein, was treated as a first priority and a decision reached prior to the acceptance of the foregoing document.

U. S. SECRET
BRITISH MOST SECRET

ABC 4
JCCSs-8
January 10, 1942.

CHIEFS OF STAFF CONFERENCE

FEDERAL RESERVE BUILDING

WASHINGTON, D. C.

3:00 P. M., JANUARY 10, 1942

Present

British Officers

   Navy

      Admiral of the Fleet, Sir Dudley Pound, First Sea Lord and Chief of Naval Staff
      Admiral Sir Charles Little, Joint Staff Mission
      Captain G. D. Belben, R.N.

   Army

      Field Marshal Sir John Dill
      Lieut. General Sir Colville Wemyss, Joint Staff Mission
      Brigadier V. Dykes, Director of Plans, War Office

   Air Force

      Air Chief Marshal Sir Charles Portal, Chief of Air Staff
      Air Marshal A. T. Harris, Joint Staff Mission

United States Officers

   Navy

      Admiral H. R. Stark, Chief of Naval Operations
      Admiral E. J. King, Commander-in-Chief, U. S. Fleet
      Rear Admiral W. R. Sexton, President, General Board
      Rear Admiral F. J. Horne, Assistant Chief of Naval Operations
      Rear Admiral J. H. Towers, Chief, Bureau of Aeronautics
      Commander R. E. Libby, Aide to Commander-in-Chief, U. S. Fleet
      Major General Thomas Holcomb, Commandant, U.S.M.C.

U. S. SECRET
BRITISH MOST SECRET

Army

    General George C. Marshall, Commanding General of the Field Forces
        and Chief of Staff
    Lt. General H. H. Arnold, Chief of the Army Air Forces and Deputy
        Chief of Staff
    Brig. General Raymond Lee, Acting Assistant Chief of Staff, G-2
    Brig. General D. D. Eisenhower, General Staff Corps

Joint Secretaries

    Brigadier L. C. Hollis, R.M.
    Colonel E. I. C. Jacob
    Captain J. L. McCrea, Aide to Chief of Naval Operations
    Lt. Colonel P. M. Robinett, G-2, GHQ
    Lt. Colonel W. T. Sexton, Assistant Secretary, W.D.G.S.

1. SUPER GYMNAST.-

ADMIRAL POUND said that the British Chiefs of Staff had made a careful examination of the various factors which affected the timing of this operation, and the earliest date on which the first convoy could arrive at Casablanca. He explained these to the Conference and undertook to let the United States Chiefs of Staff have a note on the subject. So far as the British were concerned, it appeared that if January 7 were taken as the date on which planning really began, the earliest date for D-1 on which the decision to load the first convoy could be given would be February 4. In this event the first convoy would arrive at Algiers and Casablanca on D-28, that is, March 3, depending upon the availability of shipping on that date. He also pointed out that the whole undertaking would depend upon the planning, the shipping, and the availability of troops and materiel. As to details at points of debarkation, ADMIRAL POUND said that he anticipated no difficulty in Algiers, and that in the British opinion, 29,000 men and 3,500 vehicles could be unloaded at Casablanca in the fortnight.

GENERAL MARSHALL asked Admiral Pound if the British could undertake both Casablanca and Algiers.

ADMIRAL POUND replied in the affirmative.

GENERAL MARSHALL then expressed some concern about the availability of shipping for the second convoy and undertook to confirm that January 7 could be accepted, from the American point of view, as the date on which planning began.

U. S. SECRET
BRITISH MOST SECRET

    2.   DIRECTIVE FOR THE SUPREME COMMANDER OF THE ABDA AREA - ATTITUDE OF THE DUTCH.-

ADMIRAL STARK recalled that certain amendments to Annex 2 of the draft directive for General Wavell had been proposed by the British in order to meet certain points raised by the Dutch. These had not yet been accepted by the Dutch, but had been approved by the President and the Prime Minister. He confirmed that these proposed amendments were acceptable to the United States Chiefs of Staff.

GENERAL MARSHALL said that the Dutch representative in Washington had come into the War Department a good deal over the question of the Dutch position. It appeared that the population of the Netherlands East Indies were feeling rather hurt at not having been consulted over the question of supreme command. They did not consider that the Dutch Government in London was fully representative of them. Some trouble had also been caused through the omission from General Wavell's directive of any instruction to set up his Headquarters in Java. In the original communication to the Dutch Government, which proposed the setting up of a Supreme Commander, a passage to this effect had been included.

Every endeavor had been made by BRIGADIER GENERAL GEROW to smooth down the feelings of the Dutch representative in Washington and to induce him to fall in with the agreed views of the United States and British Chiefs of Staff, but in view of the fact that negotiations with the Dutch Government were being conducted by the British, the position was somewhat embarrassing.

ADMIRAL POUND expressed the appreciation of the British Chiefs of Staff for the way in which the United States Staffs were dealing with this matter. A telegram had been sent to General Wavell instructing him to set up his Headquarters in Java, and in fact, he was establishing himself at Batavia on January 10.

THE CHIEFS OF STAFF took cognizance of the prior approval of ABC-4/5, WW 6, with Annex 2 amended, and also of the fact that further amendments would possibly be made upon reply from the Dutch and Australian Governments. (See Annex 1)

    3.   PROCEDURE FOR THE ASSUMPTION OF COMMAND BY GENERAL WAVELL.-

THE CONFERENCE had before it an amendment by the British Chiefs of Staff on the procedure for the assumption of command of General Wavell (US-ABC-4/CS-3, British WW-9). Various minor amendments were agreed to.

ADMIRAL KING suggested that it would be advisable to insert in the draft telegram to General Wavell a sentence to indicate that instructions were being sent to Admiral Hart and General Brett telling them to report to

U. S. SECRET
BRITISH MOST SECRET

him for duty in their respective posts. The following addition to the draft telegram at Annex B was accordingly agreed to:

"General Brett and Admiral Hart are being ordered by the United States Government to report to you as Deputy Supreme Commander and Commander of the Combined Naval Forces in the ABDA area respectively."

IT WAS AGREED:

    a. That the draft telegram in Annex C to the Memorandum by the British Chiefs of Staff should be dispatched forthwith. (See Annex 2)

    b. That the procedure proposed in the Memorandum should be adopted and the Memorandum, subject to the amendments agreed upon in discussion, should be approved. (See Annex 2)

4. IMMEDIATE ASSISTANCE TO CHINA.-

THE CONFERENCE had before it a memorandum received from the United States Chiefs of Staff on immediate assistance to China. (ABC-4/9, WW (J.P.C.) 9).

ADMIRAL POUND said that the British Chiefs of Staff recognized the importance of doing everything possible to facilitate assistance to China, and were in general agreement with the proposals in the paper. They wished to suggest certain amendments to it, which were designed to make it conform to the idea of Unity of Command.

THE BRITISH CHIEFS OF STAFF proposed certain amendments, which were discussed at some length.

At the suggestion of GENERAL MARSHALL the word "operate" in the fourth line of the first amendment was altered to "engage in joint operation". Similarly in the last line but one of the second amendment the words "General Wavell" were altered to "the Supreme Commander in the ABDA Area".

The following further amendment was agreed to.

On page 3, paragraph 4, line 5, the words "General Drum" were amended to read, "the United States Representative".

MARSHAL DILL suggested that the United States Representative in China might be informed of the existence and scope of the organization which had been built up in China under General Dennys. He undertook to forward a note on this point to General Marshall.

THE CONFERENCE approved the memorandum on immediate assistance to China as amended in discussion. (See Annex 3)

U. S. SECRET
BRITISH MOST SECRET

    5. POST-ARCADIA COLLABORATION.-

This paper was brought up by British Chiefs of Staff and discussed briefly. (See Annex 4)

THE CONFERENCE adjourned at 5:30 P.M., to meet at 4:00 P.M., January 11, 1942.

ENCLOSURES
    Annex 1 - Directive to Supreme Commander in the ABDA Area, US ABC-4/5, British WW-6.
    Annex 2 - Procedure for Assumption of Command by General Wavell - US-ABC-4/CS-3, British WW-9.
    Annex 3 - Immediate Assistance to China, US-ABC-4/9, British WW-10.
    Annex 4 - Post-Arcadia Collaboration, British WW-8.

U. S. SECRET
BRITISH MOST SECRET

U.S. ABC-4/5 (APPROVED)
BRITISH WW-6
(SUPERSEDES ABC-4/5, WW-3 FINAL)   January 10, 1942.

ANNEX 1
to
JCCSs-8

REPORT

BY

UNITED STATES - BRITISH

CHIEFS OF STAFF

DIRECTIVE TO THE SUPREME

COMMANDER IN THE ABDA AREA

APPROVED BY THE PRESIDENT AND THE PRIME MINISTER

U. S. SECRET
BRITISH MOST SECRET

U. S. SERIAL ABC-4/5 (APPROVED)　　　　　　　　　　　　　January 10, 1942.
BRITISH SERIAL WW-6
SUPERSEDES ABC-4/5, BRITISH WW-3 (FINAL)

DIRECTIVE TO THE SUPREME COMMANDER IN THE ABDA AREA

BY AGREEMENT AMONG THE GOVERNMENTS OF

AUSTRALIA, THE NETHERLANDS, THE UNITED

KINGDOM, AND THE UNITED STATES, HEREINAFTER

REFERRED TO AS THE ABDA GOVERNMENTS:

1. AREA.-

A strategic area has been constituted, to comprise initially all land and sea areas included in the general region Burma - Malaya - Netherlands East Indies and the Philippines; more precisely defined in Annex 1. This area will be known as the ABDA Area.

2. FORCES.-

You have been designated as the Supreme Commander of the ABDA Area and of all armed forces, afloat, ashore, and in the air, of the ABDA Governments which are or will be:-

   a. Stationed in the Area;

   b. Located in Australian territory when such forces have been allotted by the respective governments for services in or in support of the ABDA Area.

You are not authorized to transfer from the territory of any of the ABDA Governments land forces of that government without the consent of the local commander or his government.

3. The Deputy Supreme Commander and, if required, a commander of the combined naval forces and a commander of the combined air forces will be jointly designated by the ABDA Governments.

4. No government will materially reduce its armed forces assigned to your Area nor any commitments made by it for reinforcing its forces in your Area except after giving to the other governments, and to you, timely information pertaining thereto.

U. S. SECRET
BRITISH MOST SECRET

    5.   STRATEGIC CONCEPT AND POLICY.-

    The basic strategic concept of the ABDA Governments for the conduct of the war in your Area is not only in the immediate future to maintain as many key positions as possible, but to take the offensive at the earliest opportunity and ultimately to conduct an all-out offensive against Japan. The first essential is to gain general air superiority at the earliest possible moment, through the employment of concentrated air power. The piecemeal employment of air forces should be minimized. Your operations should be so conducted as to further preparations for the offensive.

    6.   THE GENERAL STRATEGIC POLICY WILL THEREFORE BE:-

    <u>a</u>.   To hold the Malay Barrier, defined as the line Malay Peninsula, Sumatra, Java, North Australia, as the basic defensive position of the ABDA Area, and to operate sea, land, and air forces in as great depth as possible forward of the Barrier in order to oppose the Japanese southward advance.

    <u>b</u>.   To hold Burma and Australia as essential supporting positions for the Area, and Burma as essential to the support of China, and to the defense of India.

    <u>c</u>.   To reestablish communications through the Dutch East Indies with Luzon and to support the Philippines' Garrison.

    <u>d</u>.   To maintain essential communications within the Area.

    7.   DUTIES, RESPONSIBILITIES, AND AUTHORITY OF THE SUPREME COMMANDER.-

    You will coordinate in the ABDA Area the strategic operations of all armed forces of the ABDA Governments; assign them strategic missions and objectives; where desirable, arrange for the formation of task forces, whether national or international, for the execution of specific operations; and appoint any officer, irrespective of seniority or nationality, to command such task forces.

    8.   While you will have no responsibilities in respect of the internal administration of the respective forces under your command, you are authorized to direct and coordinate the creation and development of administrative facilities and the broad allocation of war materials.

    9.   You will dispose reinforcements which from time to time may be dispatched to the Area by the ABDA Governments.

    10.   You are authorized to require from the Commanders of the armed forces under your command such reports as you deem necessary in the discharge of your responsibilities as Supreme Commander.

U. S. SECRET
BRITISH MOST SECRET

11. You are authorized to control the issue of all communiques concerning the forces under your command.

12. Through the channels specified in Paragraph 18, you may submit recommendations to the ABDA Governments on any matters pertaining to the furtherance of your mission.

13. LIMITATIONS.-

Your authority and control with respect to the various portions of the ABDA Area and to the forces assigned thereto will normally be exercised through the commanders duly appointed by their respective governments. Interference is to be avoided in the administrative processes of the armed forces of any of the ABDA Governments, including free communication between them and their respective governments. No alteration or revision is to be made in the basic tactical organization of such forces, and each national component of a task force will normally operate under its own commander and will not be subdivided into small units for attachment to the other national components of the task force, except in the case of urgent necessity. In general, your instructions and orders will be limited to those necessary for effective coordination of forces in the execution of your mission.

14. RELATIONS WITH ABDA GOVERNMENTS.-

The ABDA Governments will jointly and severally support you in the execution of the duties and responsibilities as herein defined, and in the exercise of the authority herein delegated and limited. Commanders of all sea, land, and air forces within your Area will be immediately informed by their respective governments that, from a date to be notified, all orders and instructions issued by you in conformity with the provisions of this directive will be considered by such commanders as emanating from their respective governments

15. In the unlikely event that any of your immediate subordinates, after making due representations to you, still considers that obedience to your orders would jeopardize the national interests of his country to an extent unjustified by the general situation in the ABDA Area, he has the right, subject to your being immediately notified of such intention, to appeal direct to his own government before carrying out the orders. Such appeals will be made by the most expeditious method, and a copy of the appeal will be communicated simultaneously to you.

16. STAFF AND ASSUMPTION OF COMMAND.-

Your staff will include officers of each of the ABDA powers. You are empowered to communicate immediately with the national commanders in the Area with a view to obtaining staff officers essential to your earliest

U. S. SECRET
BRITISH MOST SECRET

possible assumption of command. Your additional staff requirements will be communicated as soon as possible to the ABDA Governments through channels of communication described in Paragraph 18.

17. You will report when you are in a position effectively to carry out the essential functions of Supreme Command, so that your assumption of command may be promulgated to all concerned.

18. SUPERIOR AUTHORITY.-

As Supreme Commander of the ABDA Area, you will be directly responsible to the ABDA Governments through the agency defined in Annex 2.

             Signed

            (By Power furnishing
             Supreme Commander)

Countersigned:

  Other ABDA Representatives.

U. S. SECRET
BRITISH MOST SECRET

ANNEX 1
to
US - ABC-4/5

BOUNDARIES OF ABDA AREA

1. THE ABDA AREA IS BOUNDED AS FOLLOWS:

    On the North: By the boundary between India and Burma, thence eastward along the Chinese frontier and coastline to the latitude of $30°$ North, thence along the parallel of $30°$ North to the meridian of $140°$ East.

                      Note: Indo-China and Thailand are not included in this area.

    On the East: By the meridian of $140°$ East from $30°$ North, to the equator, thence east to longitude $141°$ East, thence south to the boundary of Dutch New Guinea on the South Coast, thence east along the Southern New Guinea Coast to the meridian of $143°$ East, then south down this meridian to the coast of Australia.

    On the South: By the northern coast of Australia from the meridian of $143°$ East, westward to the meridian of $114°$ East, thence northwestward to latitude $15°$ South, longitude $92°$ East.

    On the West: By the meridian of $92°$ East

2. Forces assigned to the ABDA and adjacent areas are authorized to extend their operations into other areas as may be required.

U. S. SECRET
BRITISH MOST SECRET

ANNEX 2
to
US - ABC-4/5

January 5, 1942.

HIGHER DIRECTION OF WAR IN THE ABDA AREA

1. On all important military matters, not within the jurisdiction of the Supreme Commander of the ABDA Area, the United States Chiefs of Staff and the representatives in Washington of the British Chiefs of Staff will constitute the agency for developing and submitting recommendations for decision by the President of the United States and by the British Prime Minister and Minister of Defence, on behalf of ABDA Governments. Among the chief matters on which decisions will be required are:

   a. The provision of reinforcements.

   b. A major change in policy.

   c. Departure from the Supreme Commander's directive.

2. This agency will function as follows:

   a. Any proposal coming either from the Supreme Commander or from any of the ABDA Governments will be transmitted to the Chiefs of Staff Committee both in Washington and in London.

   b. The Chiefs of Staff Committee in London having consulted the Dutch Staff, will immediately telegraph to their representatives in Washington to say whether or not they will be telegraphing any opinions.

   c. On receipt of these opinions, the United States Chiefs of Staff and the representatives in Washington of the British Chiefs of Staff will develop and submit their recommendations to the President, and by telegraph to the Prime Minister and Minister of Defence. The Prime Minister will then inform the President whether he is in agreement with these recommendations.

3. Since London has the machinery for consulting the Dominion Governments, and since the Dutch Government is in London, the British Government will be responsible for obtaining their views and agreement to every stage, and for including these in the final telegram to Washington.

U. S. SECRET
BRITISH MOST SECRET

    4.   Agreement having been reached between the President and the Prime Minister and Minister of Defence, the orders to the Supreme Commander will be dispatched from Washington in the name of the ABDA Governments and the respective governments will be fully informed.

U. S. SECRET
BRITISH MOST SECRET

U.S. ABC-4/CS-3
BRITISH WW-9 (REVISED)   January 10, 1942.

ANNEX 2
to
JCCSs-8

UNITED STATES - BRITISH

CHIEFS OF STAFF

APPROVED AS AMENDED - BRITISH CHIEFS OF STAFF

MEMORANDUM

PROCEDURE FOR ASSUMPTION OF COMMAND BY

GENERAL WAVELL

U. S. SECRET
BRITISH MOST SECRET

U.S. ABC-4 C/S 3
BRITISH WW-9 (REVISED)   January 10, 1942.

> It is requested that special
> care may be taken to insure
> the secrecy of this document.

WASHINGTON WAR CONFERENCE

PROCEDURE FOR ASSUMPTION OF COMMAND BY GENERAL WAVELL

Memorandum by British Chiefs of Staff.

1. General Wavell was informed on 29th December, 1941, by the Prime Minister that he was to be the Supreme Commander in the ABDA Area. He was told that his directive would be given to him shortly and that any observations which he might wish to make on its terms would be considered.

2. When the directive was finally approved by the President and the Prime Minister, orders were sent to London (2nd January) that it should be telegraphed to General Wavell immediately - copies were also to be sent to General Pownall and all other British Commanders concerned.

3. At the same time the terms of the directive were communicated to the Dutch, Australian, and New Zealand Governments.

4. The Dutch Government has suggested certain amendments to Annex (ii) to the directive, and these are still under discussion. It is not known whether they have communicated the directive to the Dutch Commanders in the ABDA Area.

5. The Australian Government has put forward views and opinions about the whole arrangement, and have not yet notified their agreement with the directive. It is presumed that they have not yet informed any of their Commanders.

6. The New Zealand Government is only indirectly concerned. There has been no comment on the directive from them.

7. On 2nd January General Wavell was told that much importance was attached to his taking over as soon as possible, and he was asked to specify the earliest date on which he would be ready to assume command. He is now at Singapore, but is expected to be in Batavia today, 10th January. No observations have yet been received from him about his directive, nor has he yet specified a date for assuming command.

U. S. SECRET
BRITISH MOST SECRET

8. Neither the Dutch nor the Australian Government has yet agreed to the directive, though their objections are mainly to the machinery of control laid down in Annex (ii) rather than to the directive itself. The discussions which are proceeding with those Governments may of course be successfully concluded before it becomes necessary to promulgate the date of General Wavell's appointment; but even if they are not, we do not think there need be any delay on that account. We suggest that General Wavell's appointment should be promulgated as soon as he reports he is ready, and that he should then be instructed to carry on, pending the final confirmation of his directive.

9. We accordingly propose that the following action should be taken as soon as General Wavell reports the date on which he will be ready to assume command:-

    a. His Majesty's Government should make a communication in the terms of Annex A to the Governments of the United States, The Netherlands, Australia, New Zealand, India, and China.

    b. His Majesty's Government in the United Kingdom should telegraph to General Wavell in the terms of Annex B.

    c. On receipt of the communication mentioned in a above, the Governments of the United States, The Netherlands, and Australia should at once notify their local Commanders of the date of the assumption of command by General Wavell, and should give any necessary consequential instructions so that the system planned for the ABDA Area can become effective.

    d. The terms of the directive for General Wavell, including Annex (ii), should be settled as soon as possible, and the outcome notified to all concerned.

10. We propose to telegraph home in the terms of Annex C to secure the assent of the Dutch and Australian Governments to this procedure

                                               (Signed) DUDLEY POUND.
                                                       J. G. DILL.
                                                       C. PORTAL.

Washington, D. C.

    January 10, 1942.

U. S. SECRET
BRITISH MOST SECRET

ANNEX "A"

Draft communication from His Majesty's Government in the United Kingdom to the Governments of the United States, The Netherlands, Australia, New Zealand, China, and India:

Instructions are being sent today to General Wavell that he should assume command of the ABDA Area as from January _____.

Pending final agreement between the Governments concerned on the terms of his directive and on the machinery for the higher direction of war in the ABDA Area, (Annex II to the Directive), General Wavell is being instructed to proceed in accordance with the directive as at present drafted and to communicate with Washington and London as laid down in Paragraph 18 thereof.

Please inform all Commanders concerned, accordingly.

ANNEX "B"

Draft telegram from His Majesty's Government in the United Kingdom to General Wavell:

You are to assume supreme command in the ABDA Area on January _____.

Pending final agreement between the Governments concerned on your directive, you should act in accordance with the directive sent to you in Telegram No. ____, and you should address communications to superior authority in accordance with Paragraph 18 thereof.

General Brett and Admiral Hart are being ordered by the United States Government to report to you as Deputy Supreme Commander and Commander of Combined Naval Forces, respectively, in the ABDA Area.

Governments concerned are notifying their Commanders accordingly.

U. S. SECRET
BRITISH MOST SECRET

ANNEX "C"

Draft telegram from British Chiefs of Staff to Chiefs of Staff Committee, London:

Please put following to Lord Privy Seal:

It is of highest importance that General Wavell should exercise supreme command without delay, as soon as he reports himself ready to do so.

Please propose to Dutch and Australian Governments that as soon as General Wavell reports himself as ready he should be authorized to assume command, pending the acceptance by those Governments of the ABDA machinery as set out in Annex II of his directive.

United States Chiefs of Staff agree.

U. S. SECRET
BRITISH MOST SECRET

U.S. ABC-4/9
BRITISH WW-10   January 10, 1942

                                ANNEX 3
                                  to
                                JCCSs-8

                          UNITED STATES - BRITISH

                              CHIEFS OF STAFF

                              APPROVED REPORT

                                    BY

                  UNITED STATES - BRITISH JOINT PLANNING COMMITTEE

                  U. S. SERIAL ABC-4/9, BRITISH SERIAL WW(J.P.C.)9

                          IMMEDIATE ASSISTANCE TO CHINA

U. S. SECRET
BRITISH MOST SECRET

U.S. ABC-4/9
BRITISH WW-10

January 10, 1942

JOINT PLANNING COMMITTEE REPORT

TO

CHIEFS OF STAFF

IMMEDIATE ASSISTANCE TO CHINA

1. The United States War Department has been exploring methods of increasing assistance to China so that better effect might be realized from utilization of that country's resources against Japan. Information, currently available, seems to indicate a definite and progressive weakening, morally and materially, in China's war effort. The War Department regards it as of profound importance that such steps as may be practicable and are consistent with other commitments be promptly taken to reverse this trend

2. The chief obstacle to producing a better military result in China, aside from a general scarcity of munitions, is that country's almost complete isolation. Communication with the Generalissimo is difficult and subject to delay and possible interception The long, poorly maintained, and insecure Burma Road can, at the best, support only a limited truck tonnage, -- while air raids, confusion and lack of coordination at Rangoon further limit the amounts of supplies possible to deliver to the Chinese. Several things are indicated as necessary:

    a. Closer and more effective liaison with the Generalissimo

    b. Increased security for Rangoon and the Burma Road, by air and ground.

    c. Improvement in the control, maintenance, and management of the Burma Road.

    d. Increase in base facilities and technical services.

    e. Increase in Chinese combat strength resulting from above measures.

    f. Close and effective liaison between China and the Commanding General, ABDA Area.

U. S. SECRET
BRITISH MOST SECRET

3. The War Department is considering initiation of the following steps to meet the requirements listed in Paragraph 2:

a. Arrange with the Generalissimo to accept a United States Army officer of high rank as the United States Representative in China, and to agree to the following as his functions:

(1) Supervise and control all United States Defense Aid affairs for China.

(2) Under the Generalissimo, to command all United States forces in China, and such Chinese forces as may be assigned. Should it be necessary for any of these forces to engage in joint operations in Burma, they will come under the command of the Supreme Commander of the ABDA Area, who will issue the necessary directions for the co-operation of the United States Representative's forces with the forces under the British Commanders in Burma.

(3) Represent the United States Government on any international War Council in China.

(4) Control and maintain the Burma Road, in China.

(Note: The following are projected upon the condition that *a* is, in its entirety, previously accepted by the Generalissimo.)

b. Dispatch to the South China - Burma area additional aviation strength, initially raising and maintaining the American Volunteer Group at war strength in planes and personnel. In addition, it is considered possible that several Chinese divisions may be quickly equipped for effective combat service in this area, under command of the United States Representative.

c. Arrange (with the consent of the British) for auxiliary bases in support of the Chinese effort in Burma and India, and provide the technical equipment and troops to assure the efficiency of such Rangoon facilities as are allocated to China, and to assist in the maintenance of the Burma Road.

4. To make this project reasonably effective, British cooperation and agreement are required on the points set forth hereinafter. It is understood that British agreement and cooperation will become effective only in the event that the Generalissimo accords to the United States Representatives the authority implied and indicated in Paragraph 3 *a* above.

U. S. SECRET
BRITISH MOST SECRET

POINTS ON WHICH BRITISH AGREEMENT IS SOUGHT, UNDER CONDITIONS STATED IN PARAGRAPH 3 a

    a.   In cooperation with commanders of adjacent areas, the United States Representative to be permitted to establish and/or use bases, routes, and staging areas in India and Burma to support his operations in and north of Burma.

    b.   The United States Representative to be authorized to make every effort to increase the capacity of the Burma route, throughout its length from Rangoon to Chungking. To do this he will probably be given complete executive control of the China Section of the route. On the British Section, control will still be exercised by the British authorities, both military and civil. To achieve the general aim, these British authorities will be instructed to carry out every possible improvement to the route in accordance with the requirements of the United States Representative and will accept such American technicians and equipment as may be necessary for the improvement of facilities in the Port of Rangoon and along the route itself.

    c.   The United States Representative, by arrangement with the British Commanders in Burma, to be permitted to construct and/or use necessary airfields in Burma.

    d.   The United States Representative to be accepted as the principal liaison agency between the Supreme Commander of the ABDA Area and Generalissimo Chiang Kai-shek.

U. S. SECRET
BRITISH MOST SECRET

BRITISH WW-8   January 10, 1942

ANNEX 4
to
JCCSs-8

WASHINGTON WAR CONFERENCE

POST - ARCADIA COLLABORATION

MEMORANDUM BY THE BRITISH CHIEFS OF STAFF

U. S. SECRET
BRITISH MOST SECRET

January 10, 1942

ANNEX 4
to
JCCSs-8

It is requested that special care should be taken
to insure the secrecy of this document.

WW-8
January 8, 1942.

WASHINGTON WAR CONFERENCE

POST - ARCADIA COLLABORATION

MEMORANDUM BY THE BRITISH CHIEFS OF STAFF.

    1.   We think that the United States Chiefs of Staff will wish to know what representatives of the Minister of Defence and the British Chiefs of Staff organization it is proposed to leave in Washington after the departure of the Arcadia party.

    2.   To avoid confusion, we suggest that hereafter the word "Joint" should be applied to Inter-Service collaboration and the word "Combined" to collaboration between two or more allied nations.

REPRESENTATIVE OF THE MINISTER OF DEFENCE.

    3.   Field Marshal Sir John Dill is remaining in Washington as representative of the Minister of Defence. He will have contacts with such authorities on the highest level as may be arranged between the President and the Prime Minister.

REPRESENTATIVES OF THE BRITISH CHIEFS OF STAFF.

    4.   The Heads of the Joint Staff Mission, Admiral Sir Charles Little, Lieut. General Sir Colville Wemyss, and Air Marshal A. T. Harris, will continue to represent the British Chiefs of Staff in Washington. It is hoped that a meeting between the United States Chiefs of Staff or their representatives and the representatives of the British Chiefs of Staff may be held weekly or more often if necessary. An agenda would be circulated before each meeting.

U. S. SECRET
BRITISH MOST SECRET

COMBINED PLANNING.

5. For the time being the British representatives on the Planning Staff will be -

Navy

Captain C. E. Lambe, R.N., Deputy Director of Plans, Admiralty

Army

Lieut. Colonel G. K. Bourne

R.A.F.

Group Captain S. C. Strafford

COMBINED INTELLIGENCE.

6. The arrangements for production of complete intelligence to serve the Planning Staffs are of great importance and we suggest that this matter should either be referred to the Combined Planning Staffs for report or considered by the Combined Chiefs of Staff at their next meeting.

7. We have here representatives of the Joint Intelligence Committee in London and these are available to work in conjunction with any organization the United States Chiefs of Staff may desire.

PRIORITIES AND ALLOCATION.

8. In our view, the Combined Chiefs of Staff should settle the broad programme of requirements based on strategic policy. We suggest that it will be the duty of the Combined Planning Staffs, advised by appropriate Allocation Officers, to watch, on behalf of the Combined Chiefs of Staff, the production programmes and to bring to notice instances where output does not conform to strategic policy.

9. Similarly, the Combined Chiefs of Staff should from time to time issue general directives laying down policy to govern the distribution of available weapons of war. Effect should be given to these directives by appropriate Combined Allocation Committees. These would meet periodically and make both long-term allocations (on which planning and training of forces must be based), and short-term allocations to meet immediate military needs.

10. The British representatives on the appropriate Combined Allocation Committees will for the present be -

U. S. SECRET
BRITISH MOST SECRET

<u>Navy</u>

Rear Admiral J. W. S. Dorling, R.N.

<u>Army</u>

Brigadier D. Campion

<u>R.A.F.</u>

Air Commodore E. B. C. Betts

11.   Allocation should be made as between the United States and the British Commonwealth, each caring for the needs of the Allies for whom it has accepted responsibility.

MILITARY MOVEMENTS.

12.   The Combined Chiefs of Staff would settle the broad issues of priority of overseas movement. In order to advise the Combined Chiefs of Staff and to coordinate the movement of United States and British troops and equipment so that the shipping resources of both countries are put to the best use, it appears to us that a Combined Body is desirable. The British representatives for such a body are available under Brigadier H. R. Kerr.

13.   It is suggested that this Combined Body should work in close touch with the Combined Planning Staffs through whom their advice to the Combined Chiefs of Staff would be submitted.

SECRETARIAT.

14.   A British Secretariat under Brigadier Dykes is available to serve the above organizations and to work in with any similar Secretariat system which the United States Chiefs of Staff may establish.

         (Signed) DUDLEY POUND,

          "   J. G. DILL,

          "   A. T. HARRIS,
              (for Chief of Air Staff)

Washington, D. C.,
  January 8, 1942.

U. S. SECRET
BRITISH MOST SECRET

ABC-4
JCCSs-9
January 11, 1942

THE CHIEFS OF STAFF CONFERENCE

FEDERAL RESERVE BUILDING

WASHINGTON, D. C.

4:00 P.M., January 11, 1942

Present

British Officers

    Navy

        Admiral of the Fleet Sir Dudley Pound, First Sea Lord and Chief of Naval Staff
        Admiral Sir Charles Little, Joint Staff Mission
        Captain G. D. Belben, R. N.

    Army

        Field Marshal Sir John Dill
        Lieut. General Sir Colville Wemyss, Joint Staff Mission

    Air Force

        Air Chief Marshal Sir Charles Portal, Chief of the Air Staff
        Air Marshal A. T. Harris, Joint Staff Mission

United States Officers

    Navy

        Admiral H. R. Stark, Chief of Naval Operations
        Admiral E. J. King, Commander-in-Chief, U. S. Fleet
        Rear Admiral W. R. Sexton, President, General Board
        Rear Admiral F. J. Horne, Assistant Chief of Naval Operations
        Rear Admiral J. H. Towers, Chief, Bureau of Aeronautics
        Rear Admiral R. K. Turner, Director, War Plans Division
        Major General Thomas Holcomb, Commandant, U. S. Marine Corps

U. S. SECRET
BRITISH MOST SECRET

Army

    General George C. Marshall, Commanding General of the Field Forces
        and Chief of Staff
    (Present for only part of the Conference).
    Lieut. General H. H. Arnold, Chief of the Army Air Forces and
        Deputy Chief of Staff
    Brig. General L. T. Gerow, Chief, War Plans Division
    (Present for only part of the Conference).

Joint Secretaries

    Brigadier V. Dykes, Director of Plans, War Office
    Colonel E. I. C. Jacob (Present for only part of the Conference)
    Captain J. L. McCrea, Aide to Chief of Naval Operations
    Captain F. C. Denebrink, U. S. Navy
    Lieut. Colonel P. M. Robinett, G-2, GHQ
    Lieut. Colonel W. T. Sexton, Assistant Secretary, W.D.G.S.
    Lieut. Commander R. E. Libby, Aide to Commander-in-Chief, U. S. Fleet

1.   ESTABLISHMENT OF COMMAND IN THE ABDA AREA.

    ADMIRAL POUND read to the Conference Part I of a telegram which had been received from General Wavell, in which he gave an account of a Conference held on the afternoon of 10th January, with Admiral Hart, General Brett, the Dutch Commander-in-Chief, and other commanders, and stated that he was establishing his Headquarters ten miles north of Bandoeng. Part II of the telegram had not yet been received.

    THE CONFERENCE took note of the telegram.

2.   SITUATION IN THE ABDA AREA.

    ADMIRAL STARK said that the United States Chiefs of Staff had been giving thought to the situation in the ABDA Area, which appeared to be critical. They felt that there was a good case for subordinating everything in the immediate future to the necessity for getting reinforcements quickly into that Area. Might it not be right, for example, to cut down the flow of United States troops to Northern Ireland and Iceland, if by so doing further assistance could be sent across the Pacific?

    GENERAL MARSHALL said that it was not a question of diverting troops, since these were available for both purposes. The problem was to find the necessary tonnage. The immediate necessity was to convey to Australia anti-aircraft troops, ground staff and equipment for the aircraft arriving out there, and for personnel to organize and operate the bases which must be established in Australia.

U. S. SECRET
BRITISH MOST SECRET

      THE UNITED STATES CHIEFS OF STAFF had considered whether additional shipping could be provided by cutting down the programme of reinforcements to Hawaii, but there was little to be obtained in that way, as urgent reinforcements had already been diverted to Christmas and Canton Islands, and to Samoa. The present programme of shipments of men and materiel across the Pacific would take three months, the situation being what it was. Should not the priorities over the next few weeks be weighed, with a view of deciding whether the reinforcement of ABDA could be accelerated by diverting ships from other projects, such as the moves to Iceland and Northern Ireland, and operation Super-Gymnast?

      MARSHAL DILL suggested that the best way of tackling the problem would be for the shipping experts to get together, consider total tonnage available, and see what sort of a programme could be drawn up.

      ADMIRAL STARK asked whether Singapore was in immediate danger, and how long it might be expected to hold out.

      MARSHAL DILL said that it would be a race between the arrival of reinforcements, and the progress of the Japanese. If the projected reinforcements arrived, there seemed no reason why Singapore should not hold out indefinitely. A risk had had to be taken in moving the Australian Division from the Mersing Area over to the Northwestern front, but one Indian Brigade Group had already arrived, and a British Brigade Group and 51 Hurricanes were due to arrive on 13th January.

      ADMIRAL STARK thought that if there were a chance that the race could be won, it would be worth while doing anything possible to hasten the arrival of reinforcements, and to build up the position as quickly as possible. If Singapore and the Philippines were captured by the Japanese, they would be free to bring their whole weight to bear on the Netherlands East Indies.

      GENERAL MARSHALL said that already the Japanese could move troops from the Philippines and use them for other purposes, and, in his opinion, certain indications pointed to their already being in process of doing so.

      AIR CHIEF MARSHAL PORTAL said that it would certainly be a great waste of materiel if aircraft reinforcements were poured into the ABDA Area without the necessary ground staff to operate and maintain them. He felt that before a decision was taken to sacrifice the North Atlantic move in order to provide ships for the Pacific moves, it would be well worth while holding a general review of the shipping situation. This might reveal other resources which would enable us to carry on with both projects. It should be borne in mind that the move of United States troops to Northern Ireland and Iceland was part of a chain of movements extending through the Middle East to the Far East; and he would be reluctant to see it abandoned.

U. S. SECRET
BRITISH MOST SECRET

GENERAL MARSHALL said that he did not think it would be necessary to do more than cut down the strength of the convoy which was shortly due to sail for Magnet, to approximately 10,000 men. The ships required for the Pacific move would have to be of a certain type in order to manage the long sea passage.

ADMIRAL KING inquired whether, if the North Atlantic convoy were cut so as to release personnel ships to carry 10,000 men, the urgent Pacific moves could then be accomplished.

GENERAL MARSHALL said that it would accommodate three anti-aircraft regiments badly needed in the ABDA Area; that it was not only a question of personnel ships; freight ships would also be required. That the basic problem was to accelerate movements requiring three months to consummate, into one month; those contemplated within the next few weeks to be undertaken within the next two weeks; that time - even days - is the pressing factor.

After further discussion it was agreed that the problem should be put forthwith to the British and American shipping experts, and the following terms of reference were approved:-

"To make proposals for providing shipping from United States and British resources to carry to the ABDA Area the urgent reinforcements of men and materiel which the United States Army wishes to send in the immediate future; and to show at what cost to other commitments this shipping can be found."

The above terms of reference were conveyed without delay to General Somervell, U. S. Army, and to Brigadier Napier, British Army, for immediate action.

GENERAL GEROW left the Conference in order to be present at the discussion.

3. ESTABLISHMENT OF UNITED STATES FORCES IN NORTHERN IRELAND.

THE CONFERENCE had before them a report by the Joint Planning Committee on the establishment of United States Forces in Northern Ireland. (U. S. ABC-4/7, British WW (J.P.C.) 7)

AIR CHIEF MARSHAL PORTAL referred to Paragraph 5 (c) (3) in which it was stated that it would be the responsibility of the British to provide adequate air protection and support for the United States field forces, establishments and installations in Northern Ireland. He explained that the British forces in Northern Ireland were generally protected by our own system

U. S. SECRET
BRITISH MOST SECRET

of fighter defense, the local air forces in Northern Ireland for protection and support being one night fighter squadron, two day fighter squadrons, and one Army cooperation squadron. It was proposed to make no change in these forces so long as the United States forces were not engaged in active operations, except that in some emergency it might be necessary to make a temporary reduction in the British air forces in Northern Ireland, for example, if concentrated attacks were made on convoys on the Eastern coast of England. If active operations developed in Ireland, the present British plan was to send three bomber and two fighter squadrons in addition to the air forces already there. These additions were, of course, dependent on the general situation at the time. If the main attack on the United Kingdom was being put in at some other point and an attack on Ireland were only a feint, it might not be possible to send all these additional forces. On the other hand, if the main point of danger seemed to be in Ireland, they might well be increased. He inquired whether these arrangements would be satisfactory to the American Chiefs of Staff. He did not wish them to expect a higher scale of air support than the British would be able to provide.

GENERAL ARNOLD said that the scale proposed would be acceptable to him in the circumstances.

ADMIRAL KING pointed out that since it was a matter of judgment whether the air protection and support would be "adequate", it would be more correct to change the word "adequate" to "appropriate."

THE CONFERENCE approved the report by the Joint Planning Committee (U. S. Serial ABC-4/7, British Serial WW (J.P.C.)7), subject to the substitution of the word "appropriate" for "adequate" in line 2 of paragraph 5 (c) (3). (See Annex 1.)

GENERAL MARSHALL left the Conference at this point.

4. DEFENSE OF ISLAND BASES BETWEEN HAWAII AND AUSTRALIA.

THE CONFERENCE had before them a report by the Joint Planning Committee on the defense of island bases between Hawaii and Australia. (U. S. ABC-4/8, British WW (J.P.C.)8).

GENERAL ARNOLD, referring to Paragraph 9 (d), questioned the advisability of sending air forces to New Caledonia "even if this has to be at the expense, initially, of the ABDA Area." Even if shipping were available there were not available a pursuit squadron and a medium bomber squadron to be sent immediately except at the expense of the ABDA Area. He did not think that New Caledonia should have priority over Fiji or Samoa. Samoa was of particular importance, since if it were lost the air route for the heavy bombers from America to the ABDA Area would be cut.

U. S. SECRET
BRITISH MOST SECRET

ADMIRAL KING pointed out that New Caledonia was of great importance to the ABDA Area. Not only were the nickel mines a tempting bait for the Japanese, but also if the Island was in Japanese possession, all reinforcements to the ABDA Area would have to take the long route south of New Zealand.

GENERAL HOLCOMB said that the garrison proposed for Samoa (in the Annex to the paper) was already en route. There was no question of diverting any part of it.

ADMIRAL POUND suggested that the shipping experts who were examining the possibility of providing additional shipping for reinforcing the ABDA Area should be instructed to take into account the needs of New Caledonia and see if it were not possible to send in the necessary reinforcements without taking anything away from what was proposed for the ABDA Area itself. General Gerow was notified of this.

GENERAL ARNOLD pointed out that shipping was the limiting factor only for the land forces; in the case of air forces, it was availability.

After some discussion it was agreed that the first sentence of Paragraph 9 (d) should be amended to read as follows:-

"That the defense of New Caledonia should, in principle, be accepted as an Australian responsibility, but that the United States should, as a temporary measure, furnish forces for the defense of the Island immediately after meeting the emergency in the ABDA Area."

ADMIRAL KING said that the following addition should be made to Column (c) of the Annex under Item 3, Samoa:-

1 Fighter Squadron
1 Dive Bomber Squadron

ADMIRAL TURNER explained that reference had been made to the need for obtaining from Australia an opinion as to the priority for arming the Free French on the Island because there was some doubt whether, in view of the shortage of equipment and shipping, these troops were worth arming at the expense of other requirements in, say, Australia. It had not been intended by the Joint Planning Committee that these forces should never be armed at all.

U. S. SECRET
BRITISH MOST SECRET

THE CONFERENCE:-

<u>a</u> Accepted, in principle, the report of the Joint Planning Committee (U. S. ABC-4/8, British WW (J.P.C.)8), subject to confirmation by General Marshall, and to the amendments agreed in the discussion.

<u>b</u> Invited the British Chiefs of Staff:-

(1) To obtain without delay from Australia an opinion as to the priority for arming the 3,700 Free French in New Caledonia;

(2) To take up immediately with the Free French the question of the demolition, if necessary, of the furnaces and power plant of the nickel mines, and the loading facilities for chrome and nickel ore in New Caledonia.

<u>c</u> Agreed that the American and British shipping experts should be instructed to include in the examination which they had been ordered to carry out (vide Minute 2) the possibility of sending urgent reinforcements from America to New Caledonia, without retarding the rate of reinforcing the ABDA Area itself.

5. INCLUSION OF PORT DARWIN IN THE ABDA AREA.

ADMIRAL POUND said that a telegram had been received from General Wavell pointing out that it was not clear whether Port Darwin was included in the ABDA Area as defined in his directive or not. He felt that it should be, since it was linked up with the control of the Timor Sea, which was his responsibility. The British Chiefs of Staff agreed that there was more to be considered than the mere local defense of the port, but Australia would, of course, have to be consulted. It appeared that since Port Darwin was an essential base of the ABDA Area, the case might be covered by Paragraph 2 of the directive, which placed General Wavell in command of forces "located in Australian territory when such forces have been allotted by the respective Governments for services in or IN SUPPORT OF the ABDA Area."

ADMIRAL STARK expressed, on behalf of the American Chiefs of Staff, the opinion that the defense of Port Darwin should be made the responsibility of General Wavell, in view of the fact that it was a necessary base for the ABDA Area.

The Conference adjourned at 6:00 P.M., to meet at 2:00 P.M., January 12, 1942.

ENCLOSURES
  Annex 1 - Establishment of United States Forces in Northern Ireland (U. S. ABC-4/7, British WW-12).

U. S. SECRET
BRITISH MOST SECRET

ANNEX 1
to
JCCSs-9

U. S. SERIAL ABC-4/7   Washington, D. C.
   (APPROVED)
BRITISH SERIAL WW-12   January 11, 1942

UNITED STATES - BRITISH

CHIEFS OF STAFF

APPROVED

REPORT BY THE UNITED STATES - BRITISH

JOINT PLANNING COMMITTEE

U. S. ABC-4/7   British WW-12

ESTABLISHMENT OF UNITED STATES FORCES IN NORTH IRELAND

U. S. SECRET
BRITISH MOST SECRET

U. S. SERIAL ABC-4/7   Washington, D. C.
BRITISH SERIAL WW (JPC) 7   January 10, 1942.

ESTABLISHMENT OF UNITED STATES FORCES IN NORTH IRELAND

1. MISSION.

United States Army troops will be dispatched to North Ireland for the accomplishment of the following missions:

    a   To relieve the mobile elements of the British forces in North Ireland and, in cooperation with British local defense forces, to defend North Ireland against attack by Axis Powers.

    b   To be prepared to move into South Ireland for the defense thereof.

2. FORCES.

The forces which will be employed are the V Army Corps, consisting of the 32d, 34th, 37th Divisions, Corps Troops, Army and Corps Service Elements, with the 1st Armored Division attached. This force is under the command of Major General Edmund L. Daley, U. S. Army. The strength of the field forces, less aviation and auxiliary units and anti-aircraft units, is approximately 105,000 officers and men, for which approximately 1,207,500 ship tons are required. The strength of the anti-aircraft personnel (to be provided later) is approximately 31,000 officers and men. The strength of aviation and auxiliary personnel is approximately 22,000 officers and men. Movement of air units can commence on or about February 1, 1942, if shipping is available. When the air and anti-aircraft support is assumed by the United States forces, an additional 583,000 ship tons will be required.

3. COMMAND.

Command of all United States Army forces and personnel in the British Isles, including those in North Ireland, is vested in Major General James E. Chaney, who has been designated, "Commander United States Army Forces in the British Isles." The term "command" is defined as that control of individuals, forces, functions, and establishments which is normally vested in, and exercised by, United States Army commanders by law, regulations, and competent orders. General Chaney is authorized to arrange with appropriate British authorities for the employment:

    (1)   of organizations of his command under British control, and

    (2)   of British organizations under United States control.

U. S. SECRET
BRITISH MOST SECRET

4. STRATEGIC DIRECTION.

a The strategic direction of the United States Army Forces in the British Isles will be exercised by the British Government through the Commander, United States Army Forces in the British Isles.

b The term "strategic direction" is defined to mean the function of prescribing for a force as a whole the general mission which it is to carry out over a long period of time, and such modifications of that general mission as may from time to time become necessary or desirable, without any control of details of tactical operations or administrative matters.

c It is agreed however that units assigned to the United States North Ireland Force will not be moved to areas outside Ireland without prior consent of the Commanding General, Field Forces, United States Army.

5. ARRANGEMENTS FOR THE OPERATION.

The following agreements in respect to arrangements for the operation have been arrived at:

a Questions relative to despatch of United States Army Forces and materials from the United States that may require British collaboration will be handled through the British Mission in the United States.

b Matters connected with command, reception, distribution, accommodation and maintenance of the United States Army Forces in Northern Ireland that may require collaboration between the two governments will be handled for the United States through the Commander, United States Forces in the British Isles.

c WEAPONS AND EQUIPMENT

(1) ANTI-AIRCRAFT. Initially all anti-aircraft protection for United States Field Forces, establishments and installations will be the responsibility of the British. Eventually anti-aircraft protection for United States forces in Northern Ireland will be provided from United States personnel equipped and maintained for armament and ammunition from British sources.

(2) FIELD ARTILLERY. Initially 144 25-pounders, with 1500 rounds per gun, will be delivered by the British to United States Forces in Northern Ireland. The British will supply additional ammunition and maintenance equipment for these weapons as requested by the Commander, United States Forces in the British Isles.

U. S. SECRET
BRITISH MOST SECRET

        (3) AIR. It will be the responsibility of the British to provide appropriate air protection and support for the United States Field Forces, establishments and installations in Northern Ireland, in their mission, until such time as the means are made available to the Commander, United States Forces in the British Isles, to assume this responsibility.

    <u>d</u>   SHELTER.

    It will be the responsibility of the British to provide shelter for the United States Army Forces in Northern Ireland.

U. S. SECRET
BRITISH MOST SECRET

ABC-4
JCCSs-10

January 12, 1942

CHIEFS OF STAFF CONFERENCE

FEDERAL RESERVE BUILDING

WASHINGTON, D. C.

4:00 P.M., JANUARY 12, 1942

Present

British Officers

    Navy

        Admiral of the Fleet, Sir Dudley Pound, First Sea Lord and Chief of Naval Staff
        Admiral Sir Charles Little, Joint Staff Mission

    Army

        Field Marshal Sir John Dill
        Lieut. General Sir Colville Wemyss, Joint Staff Mission
        Brigadier C. S. Napier, British War Office

    Air Force

        Air Chief Marshal Sir Charles Portal, Chief of Air Staff
        Air Marshal A. T. Harris, Joint Staff Mission

United States Officers

    Navy

        Admiral H. R. Stark, Chief of Naval Operations
        Admiral E. J. King, Commander-in-Chief, U. S. Fleet
        Rear Admiral W. R. Sexton, President, General Board
        Rear Admiral F. J. Horne, Assistant Chief of Naval Operations
        Rear Admiral J. H. Towers, Chief, Bureau of Aeronautics
        Rear Admiral R. K. Turner, Director, War Plans Division
        Major General Thomas Holcomb, Commandant, U.S.M.C.

U. S. SECRET
BRITISH MOST SECRET

Army

General George C. Marshall, Commanding General of the Field Forces
and Chief of Staff
Lt. General H. H. Arnold, Chief of the Army Air Forces and Deputy
Chief of Staff
Brig. General L. T. Gerow, Chief, War Plans Division

Joint Secretaries

Brigadier V. Dykes, Director of Plans, War Office
Brigadier L. C. Hollis, R.M.
Captain J. L. McCrea, Aide to Chief of Naval Operations
Captain F. C. Denebrink, U.S.N.
Lt. Commander R. E. Libby, Aide to Commander-in-Chief, U. S. Fleet
Lt. Colonel P. M. Robinett, G-2 GHQ
Lt. Colonel W. T. Sexton, Assistant Secretary, W.D.G.S.

1.   SHIPPING FOR UNITED STATES REINFORCEMENTS FOR THE FAR EAST.-

GENERAL MARSHALL gave the Conference an outline of certain proposals which had been submitted by the United States Staffs for expediting the move of American reinforcements to the Pacific and ABDA Area. (See Annex 1) He explained that these proposals had been developed since the meeting of United States and British shipping experts on the previous evening. If the proposals were accepted, it would be possible to sail a convoy of 21,800 men from New York for the Far East on January 20. Of this, some 10,000 were earmarked for the defense of New Caledonia, the remainder being ground staffs for air squadrons. The effect would be to reduce the Iceland convoy sailing on January 5 from 8,000 to 2,500, and the Northern Ireland convoy from 16,000 to 4,000. Certain additional American ships not at present scheduled for troop movements would also be employed, such as ships on the South American trade, and train ferries.

BRIGADIER NAPIER said that the proposal for the QUEEN MARY to take American troops to the United Kingdom and pick up a load there for the Middle East was a new idea which he had not yet had time to study. At the shipping conference the proposal had been that she should take troops from New York to South Africa for onward carriage in the United States ships WEST POINT and WAKEFIELD across the Indian Ocean. The proposal that the MOUNT VERNON, WAKEFIELD and WEST POINT should be left in the Indian Ocean for a second round trip from the Middle East to the Far East was also new. London had already arranged an Indian Ocean convoy program which excluded these ships, in order that they should revert to American use, and must be consulted as to their most useful employment.

U. S. SECRET
BRITISH MOST SECRET

SIR CHARLES PORTAL inquired whether the shipment of some 400 aircraft to the Far East would cut into American aircraft replacements to the Middle East. It seemed very probable that there would be intensive air operations in the near future in the Mediterranean, and the rate of attrition there was likely to be much more heavy than in the Pacific, where air operations were sporadic and on a comparatively light scale. In these circumstances, he would not be able to agree to any diversion from the Middle East. It was the P-40 and Martin 187 Baltimores in which he was particularly interested.

GENERAL ARNOLD, after inquiry, confirmed that the proposed program would not interfere with the dispatch of replacement aircraft of the P-40 and Martin 187 types to the Middle East.

GENERAL MARSHALL pointed out that the reinforcements proposed would involve a cut of up to 30 per cent in monthly deliveries to Russia. This would be in addition to a certain deficiency which was already likely to arise on the program of supplies to Russia up to April 1, 1942. The ships involved in the United States reinforcement program would be diverted from carrying supplies to Russia for a period of up to four months.

SIR JOHN DILL said that undoubtedly there would be considerable pressure on political grounds not to cut down Russian supplies in any way.

ADMIRAL KING pointed out that it was doubtful whether the Russians could clear the full amount of supplies which were delivered to them. In so far as this was the case, therefore, a cut in deliveries would be of no consequence.

SIR JOHN DILL said that the effect of the proposed program, so far as Ireland was concerned, appeared to be a postponement of the arrival of some 20,000 troops by one month. In the case of Iceland, the rate of relief of British troops and the United States Marines would be cut down to about 2,500 per month. He thought these reductions could be accepted in view of the urgent needs of the Far East. A token force of some 4,000, at least, would be going to Northern Ireland and that was of great political significance.

BRIGADIER NAPIER inquired whether, if 21,800 men were sailed from New York on January 20 in the ships which were loading for Iceland and Ireland, they would not arrive in the Pacific Area before their equipment, which would have moved in slower freight ships. He had had this consideration in mind when suggesting that the QUEEN MARY should take United States personnel to South Africa for onward carriage after she had finished docking in New York. Under this arrangement the troops would have arrived about the same time as their equipment.

GENERAL MARSHALL said that it seemed important to rush in personnel in one convoy, if possible, in order to simplify the escort problem. Moreover, it was likely to be easier to get the troops through without enemy interference

U. S. SECRET
BRITISH MOST SECRET

if it were done earlier rather than later. It might be necessary to accept the fact that the personnel would arrive without all of their equipment. At the present time the only American forces in Australia were the ground staff for one bomber group with a certain number of pilots, and an artillery brigade which had no ammunition. Ammunition and a certain amount of equipment for this brigade were due to arrive there almost immediately.

In his view, the whole question was one of priorities. For example, was the dispatch of some 10,000 troops for New Caledonia of greater strategic importance than the relief of British troops in Northern Ireland, or supplies to Russia? An immediate decision was necessary on the Ireland and Iceland shipping, since ships already loading in New York would have to be unloaded and re-stowed if they were to get away on January 20.

Admiral Stark summed up the effect of General Marshall's proposals as follows:

a. They would set back the relief of Northern Ireland by one month.

b. The Middle and Near East would not be affected.

c. The supply and Lend-Lease materials to Russia would be reduced by 30% for a period of three to four months.

d. The situation in the Far East would be immeasurably strengthened.

After some discussion it was generally agreed that the postponement of the dispatch of some 20,000 troops to Northern Ireland by one month and the reduction in the rate of relief of the troops in Iceland could be accepted, but that there should be no interference with the supply of American aircraft to the Middle East. The crux of the position, therefore, was whether a cut of up to 30 per cent in monthly deliveries to Russia could be accepted for a period probably of four months.

THE CONFERENCE:

a. Agreed that the provisional program as outlined by General Marshall would have to be referred to the President and the Prime Minister for a ruling on the question of interruption of Russian supplies;

b. That, before the proposals for the use of the QUEEN MARY and the three United States ships in the Indian Ocean could be accepted, it would be necessary to consult the British Shipping Authorities in

U. S. SECRET
BRITISH MOST SECRET

London in order to insure that convoy programs already worked out were not upset, and that shipping was used in the most economical manner.

2. DEFENSE OF ISLAND BASES BETWEEN HAWAII AND AUSTRALIA.-

GENERAL MARSHALL signified his acceptance of the report of the Joint Planning Committee on the defense of island bases between Hawaii and Australia (U.S. ABC-4/8, British WW (J.P.C.)8) subject to the amendments which had been agreed to in discussion at the previous meeting. (See Annex 2)

ENCLOSURES
    Annex 1 - Memorandum of Proposed Shipping Adjustments.
    Annex 2 - Defense of Island Bases between Hawaii and Australia (U.S. ABC-4/8, British WW-13)

U. S. SECRET
BRITISH MOST SECRET

January 12, 1942

ANNEX 1
to
JCCSs-10

MEMORANDUM OF PROPOSED SHIPPING ADJUSTMENTS

U. S. SECRET
BRITISH MOST SECRET

ANNEX 1
to
JCCSs-10

MEMORANDUM OF PROPOSED SHIPPING ADJUSTMENTS

    IRELAND

        Reduce present plan for sailing January 15 of 16,000 as follows:

            4,100 troops to sail January 15
            7,000 troops on QUEEN MARY to sail February 1
            9,000 troops on ANDES, ORONZAY, and ORION, to sail February 15-20
            4,400 troops on GEORGE WASHINGTON to sail February 24.

Total .. 24,500 to sail January 15 to February 24.

        (Note: Cargo tonnage extremely short. British must provide shelter, or lumber to winterize tents).

    ICELAND

        Reduce present plan for sailing January 15 of 8,000 as follows:

            2,500 troops on January 15.

        (Note: Remainder as shipping becomes available. Probably about 2,500 per month.)

    BRITISH TROOPS

        NEAR EAST AND FAR EAST

            7,000 on QUEEN MARY to load in England.
            5,100 from Cairo on MOUNT VERNON - now in Far East.
            11,200 from Cairo on second round trip of WEST POINT and WAKEFIELD - Now engaged in first round trip for Far East.

Total .. 23,300 British troops for Near and Far East on United States ships and QUEEN MARY.

- 1 -

U. S. SECRET
BRITISH MOST SECRET

UNITED STATES TROOPS

FAR EAST

21,800 troops, to sail from New York January 20.

- 250 Pursuit planes
- 86 Medium Bombers
- 57 Light Bombers

228,000 Cargo Tons.

4-1/2 million gallons of gasoline.

(Note: Troops are air and supporting services, except for a reinforced brigade for New Caledonia of 10,000 men).

U. S. SECRET
BRITISH MOST SECRET

U.S. SERIAL ABC-4/8 (APPROVED)　　　　　　　　　　　　January 13, 1942.
BRITISH SERIAL WW-13

ANNEX 2
to
JCCSs-10

UNITED STATES - BRITISH

CHIEFS OF STAFF

APPROVED

REPORT BY THE UNITED STATES - BRITISH

JOINT PLANNING COMMITTEE

DEFENSE OF ISLAND BASES

BETWEEN HAWAII AND AUSTRALIA

U. S. SECRET
BRITISH MOST SECRET

U.S. SERIAL ABC-4/8
BRITISH SERIAL WW (J.P.C.)8

January 10, 1942.

JOINT PLANNING COMMITTEE

REPORT FOR THE CHIEFS OF STAFF

COMMITTEE

DEFENSE OF ISLAND BASES

BETWEEN HAWAII AND AUSTRALIA

    1.   There is under development and approaching completion, an air route suitable for the use of both long and medium range aircraft and extending from Hawaii to Australia. Airdromes are located at Palmyra, Christmas, Canton, American Samoa, Fiji, and New Caledonia. In addition to their use as staging points along the air route, all of these islands are valuable outposts of the defenses of the Hawaiian Islands or of New Zealand and Australia. They will serve also as operating bases for naval and air forces.

    2.   In addition to its military importance, New Caledonia is an important Japanese objective, since it is the principal readily accessible source of supply for nickel, of which the Japanese have at present only a limited supply. At present the total output of nickel is shipped to the United States. In emergency this source of supply could be denied to the Japanese for some time by the destruction of the blast furnaces, power supply, and limited loading facilities.

    3.   It is planned also to establish at Borabora, in the Society Islands, which are under Free French jurisdiction, a base for refuelling naval vessels and other shipping en route to and from the Southwest Pacific.

    4.   The defense of all the island positions along the route, depends ultimately upon their support by naval and air forces. The final strength of forces recommended herein is based on the length of time which in present circumstances may elapse before naval and air support can be made effective. The strength of the forces required will have to be kept under constant review. In the present situation, the Japanese appear to be able to attack New Caledonia or Fiji at an early date with a force of at least one infantry division, supported by strong naval and air forces.

    5.   The present garrisons of the island bases are inadequate to hold out unsupported against the attacks of which the Japanese are capable. The degree

U. S. SECRET
BRITISH MOST SECRET

of resistance to the Japanese of the French and native troops in New Caledonia is unknown.

6. The United States is able to provide forces for the defense of Palmyra, Christmas, Canton, American Samoa, and Borabora.

7. New Zealand is sending most of the personnel needed for the defense of Viti Levu. The United States already is providing one pursuit squadron and very considerable quantities of the equipment required for the Fijis. The remainder is being supplied from British sources. Most of the equipment needed will be supplied in the near future.

8. Although we consider that New Caledonia should be an Australian responsibility, we are informed that, owing to the scarcity of troops for home defense in the absence of four divisions overseas, Australia is unable to increase the small garrison of one company now in New Caledonia within the next six months. Australia is laying minefields in the approaches to Noumea and Tontouta. We consider that it is important to provide more adequate defenses in the island as early as possible. The only way to do this would be for the United States to send the necessary forces. These would, however, initially be at the expense of the ABDA Area. An opinion should also be obtained from Australia as to the priority for arming the 3700 Free French on the island. A list has been received of their requirements.

RECOMMENDATIONS

9. *a*. That the United States arrange for the local defense of Palmyra, Christmas, Canton, American Samoa, and Borabora. This is now being accomplished.

b. That the Dominion of New Zealand be responsible for the local defense of the Fiji Islands.

c. That the United States assist in providing equipment and air defenses for the Fiji Islands.

d. That the defense of New Caledonia should in principle be accepted as an Australian responsibility, but that the United States should as a temporary measure, furnish forces as early as possible for the defense of the island, immediately after meeting the emergency in the ABDA Area. The question of arming the Free French troops should be taken up between the United States and British Staffs as soon as an opinion has been obtained from Australia as to the priority.

e. Arrangements should be made immediately by the British with the Free French for the demolition, if necessary, of the furnaces and power plant

U. S. SECRET
BRITISH MOST SECRET

of the nickel mines and the loading facilities for chrome and nickel ore in New Caledonia.

    f. That Australia and New Zealand afford all practicable logistic support to United States forces which may be assigned to assist in the defense of the Fijis and New Caledonia.

    g. The attached table shows forces present in the islands, or en route, and those we recommend should be sent in the future as shipping and naval escorts become available.

U. S. SECRET
BRITISH MOST SECRET

ANNEX TO ABC-4/8

DEFENSE OF ISLAND BASES

BETWEEN HAWAII AND AUSTRALIA

PLACE	DEFENSES NOW THERE OR EN ROUTE	ESTIMATED DESIRABLE GARRISON TO BE COMPLETED AS FORCES, NAVAL ESCORT, AND SHIPPING BECOME AVAILABLE (Includes Col. (b))	REMARKS
(a)	(b)	(c)	(d)
1. NEW CALEDONIA	One Co. A.I.F. Approximately 3,000 Free French Forces (inadequately equipped) 2 6" Fixed Defense Guns (Free French)	Army 1 Inf. Division (4 regiments) 24 Heavy A.A. guns. 48 Light A.A. guns. 24 .50 Calibre A.A. M.G.'s 12 A.A. Searchlights 8 155 m.m. C.A. guns 1 Eng. Regt. (Gen. Serv.) Air 1 Pursuit Sq. (25 aircraft) 1 Medium Bomb. Sq. (13 aircraft) Air Warning Service. Approximate Total Strength 40,000. See Notes (a) and (b) in Col. (d).	Note (a). Does not include Free French Forces. This island is 230 miles long and 30 miles wide. Force envisages protection of the 3 to 4 air fields, and, in the southern half of the island, the harbor of Noumea. Note (b). The size of the garrison is subject to review as a result of early reconnaissance and degree of assistance afforded by Free French; latter entails completing re-equipment of Free French.

- 1 -

U. S. SECRET
BRITISH MOST SECRET

ANNEX TO ABC-4/8

PLACE	DEFENSES NOW THERE OR EN ROUTE	ESTIMATED DESIRABLE GARRISON TO BE COMPLETED AS FORCES, NAVAL ESCORT, AND SHIPPING BECOME AVAILABLE (Includes Col. (b))	REMARKS
(a)	(b)	(c)	(d)
2. FIJI	Naval 1 Minesweeper 4 Motor Patrol Boats Army 6 New Zealand Inf. Bns. 1 Regular Fiji Bn. (1/8 European) 1 Territorial Fiji Bn. (1/3 European) 28 Field Guns 2 6" C.A. guns at Momi 2 6" C.A. guns at Suva 2 4.7" C.A. guns at Suva 2 60 Pounders 2 6" Howitzers 4 Bofors 4 3" A.A. guns 6 A.A. Searchlights Air 9 Reconnaissance Bombers* 9 Miscellaneous Aircraft* 4 Singapore Flying Boats 700 Men, Air Corps) 25 Airplanes,) U.S. Fighters) 2 sets RADAR	Naval 1 Minesweeper 8 Motor Patrol Boats Army 8 Inf. Bns. 16 Heavy A.A. guns 28 Light A.A. guns 12 .50 Cal. A.A. M.G.'s. 12 A.A. Searchlights 2 C.A. 155 m.m. guns for Momi 4 6" C.A. guns at Momi and Suva 2 4.7" C.A. guns at Suva 2 60 Pounders 2 6" Howitzers 28 Field Guns 1 Co. Tanks (L) (13 Tanks) Air 1 Pursuit (I) Squad. (25 Aircraft) 1 Medium Bombardment Squad. (16 Aircraft) 1 Flying Boat Squad. (8 Aircraft) 4 Sets RADAR	Air U.S. Army is supplying the pursuit squadron. *Obsolete. Should be replaced by Hudsons due to New Zealand under approved allocations.

- 2 -

U. S. SECRET
BRITISH MOST SECRET

ANNEX TO ABC-4/8

PLACE	DEFENSES NOW THERE OR EN ROUTE	ESTIMATED DESIRABLE GARRISON TO BE COMPLETED AS FORCES, NAVAL ESCORT, AND SHIPPING BECOME AVAILABLE (Includes Col.(b))	REMARKS
(a)	(b)	(c)	(d)

3. SAMOA	4 6" guns
	18 3" A.A. guns
	42 .50 M.G's.
	42 .30 M.G's.
	415 Marines
	150 Samoan Marines
	1 Regiment of Marines
	12 75 m.m. guns
	1 Co. Light Tanks (13 Tanks)
	Hq. Troops
	6 5" guns
	Total - 5,015 U.S. Marines
	6 Scout observation seaplanes (Navy)
	2 Sets RADAR
		As in column (b)
		1 Fighter Squadron (By
		1 Dive Bomber U. S.
		  Squadron Ma-
		                rines)	

4. CANTON	45 Engineers 10 Medical and Communication 10 Artillery Personnel 2 75 m.m. guns 12 Machine guns	2 Cos. Inf. Rifle 4 guns C.A. A.A. (90 m.m.) 8 guns C.A. A.A. (37 m.m.) 12 Cal. .50 A.A. M.G's. 2 75 m.m. guns 2 5" Cal. .51 Navy guns 8 37 m.m. A/T guns 2 5" Navy guns 1 Pursuit Squadron (25 Aircraft) 2 RADAR	

U. S. SECRET
BRITISH MOST SECRET

ANNEX TO ABC-4/8

PLACE	DEFENSES NOW THERE OR EN ROUTE	ESTIMATED DESIRABLE GARRISON TO BE COMPLETED AS FORCES, NAVAL ESCORT, AND SHIPPING BECOME AVAILABLE (Includes Col. (b))	REMARKS
(a)	(b)	(c)	(d)
5. CHRISTMAS ISLAND	125 Engineers, Medical and Signal Personnel 10 Artillery Personnel 12 Machine Guns 4 3" A.A. Guns 2 75 m.m. Guns 2 155 m.m. Guns	1 Bn. Inf. 4 guns C.A. A.A. (90 m.m.) 8 guns C.A. A.A. (37 m.m.) 12 Cal. .50 M.G's. A.A. 2 75 m.m. guns 2 5" Cal. .51 Navy guns 5 searchlights 1 Pursuit Sqdn. (25 aircraft) 2 Sets, RADAR	
6. PALMYRA	479 Marines 4 5" guns 4 3" A.A. guns 8 .50 A.A. Machine Guns 8 .30 A.A. Machine Guns 2 Sets, RADAR	As in column (b) 1 Pursuit Squadn. (25 aircraft)	Certain other equipment now installed, details of which are not now available.
7. BORABORA	NONE	1 Inf. Regt. (- 2 Bns.) 12 guns A.A. (90 m.m.) 24 guns A.A. (37 m.m.) 24 Cal. .50 M.G's. 8 guns (75 m.m.) 2 CA Btrys. (Harbor Defense) 6 Scout observation seaplanes (Navy) Services	

U. S. SECRET
BRITISH MOST SECRET

ABC-4
JCCSs-11

January 13, 1942

CHIEFS OF STAFF CONFERENCE

FEDERAL RESERVE BUILDING

WASHINGTON, D. C.

4:00 P.M., JANUARY 13, 1942

Present

British Officers

    Navy

        Admiral of the Fleet Sir Dudley Pound, First Sea Lord and Chief of Naval Staff
        Admiral Sir Charles Little, Joint Staff Mission

    Army

        Field Marshal Sir John Dill
        Lieut. General Sir Colville Wemyss, Joint Staff Mission

    Air Force

        Air Chief Marshal Sir Charles Portal, Chief of Air Staff
        Air Marshal A. T. Harris, Joint Staff Mission

United States Officers

    Navy

        Admiral H. R. Stark, Chief of Naval Operations
        Admiral E. J. King, Commander-in-Chief, U. S. Fleet
        Rear Admiral W. R. Sexton, President, General Board
        Rear Admiral F. J. Horne, Assistant Chief of Naval Operations
        Rear Admiral J. H. Towers, Chief, Bureau of Aeronautics
        Rear Admiral R. K. Turner, Director, War Plans Division
        Major General Thomas Holcomb, Commandant, U. S. Marine Corps

U. S. SECRET
BRITISH MOST SECRET

    Army

        General George C. Marshall, Commanding General of the Field Forces
            and Chief of Staff
        Lieut. General H. H. Arnold, Chief of the Army Air Forces and
            Deputy Chief of Staff
        Brig. General L. T. Gerow, Chief, War Plans Division

Joint Secretaries

        Brigadier V. Dykes
        Brigadier L. C. Hollis, R. M.
        Captain J. L. McCrea, Aide to Chief of Naval Operations
        Captain F. C. Denebrink, U. S. N.
        Lieut. Commander R. E. Libby, Aide to Commander-in-Chief, U. S. Fleet
        Lieut. Colonel P. M. Robinett, G-2, GHQ
        Lieut. Colonel W. T. Sexton, Assistant Secretary, W.D.G.S.

1. POST-ARCADIA COLLABORATION.

THE CONFERENCE had before them a memorandum by the British Chiefs of Staff on Post-Arcadia Collaboration (WW-8).

SIR DUDLEY POUND said that the arrangements for collaboration on the operational side proposed in the paper would be suitable not only for ABDA, but for all other operational matters as well. The question of intelligence was closely bound up with planning, and this aspect was also dealt with in the paper. As regards the allocation of war materiel, the British Chiefs of Staff felt that if we were to get the best use out of our resources, allocation must be made on strategical grounds in accordance with general directives issued by the Combined Chiefs of Staff. America and Great Britain would each take on certain groups of Associated Nations and, after receiving bulk allocations from United States and British production, would sub-allocate them among their own groups.

THE CONFERENCE then considered the paper paragraph by paragraph.

It was agreed that Paragraph 2 would be better worded as follows:

    "2. To avoid confusion we suggest that hereafter the word 'Joint' should be applied to Inter-Service collaboration of ONE NATION and the word 'Combined' to collaboration between two or more UNITED NATIONS".

U. S. SECRET
BRITISH MOST SECRET

ADMIRAL STARK, referring to Paragraph 3, said that the United States Chiefs of Staff felt that if anyone could carry out the duties laid down therein, they would rather have Sir John Dill than anyone else. They felt strongly, however, that there should be no Military Representative of the British Government above the Chiefs of Staff level. They would not desire for a moment to have any similar arrangement in London whereby a Military Representative of the United States had direct access to higher political authority. He thought it only right to express the views of the United States Chiefs of Staff quite frankly on this matter, though he realized that the President and the Prime Minister might have come to some other agreement on the matter.

SIR DUDLEY POUND said that the British Chiefs of Staff would have to refer the matter to the Prime Minister, as any decision on this point would have to be taken on a higher level.

ADMIRAL STARK said that the United States Chiefs of Staff accepted, without comment, Paragraphs 4 and 5 of the paper, but in Paragraph 6 would like to have the following amendments made:

Line 4 - delete "either".

Lines 5 and 6 - delete "or considered by the Combined Chiefs of Staff at their next meeting".

The principle that coordinated intelligence should be available for the Planning Staffs was fully accepted, but the details would have to be worked out by the Planning Staffs in collaboration.

As regards Paragraphs 8 to 11 (Priorities and Allocation), the UNITED STATES CHIEFS OF STAFF entirely agreed with the principle enunciated in the first sentence of Paragraph 8. The United States organization for allocation was not, however, yet in final shape, and before accepting the remainder of these paragraphs, they would like to examine the matter further.

SIR DUDLEY POUND suggested that the principle involved in this matter was so important that it would be desirable for the Combined Chiefs of Staff to submit their recommendations to the President and the Prime Minister.

A draft minute was handed round for discussion and agreed to, subject to certain amendments. A copy of the agreed minute is attached to Annex 1.

GENERAL MARSHALL in this discussion emphasized that there could be no question of having any duplication of the Combined Chiefs of Staff organization in Washington and in London. There could only be one Combined

U. S. SECRET
BRITISH MOST SECRET

Chiefs of Staff who would give broad directions on the allocation of materiel. He saw no objection whatever to having parallel Allocation Committees in Washington and London, dealing with the allocation of American and British war materiel respectively.

The discussion then turned on the control of shipping dealt with in Paragraph 12.

GENERAL MARSHALL felt that the Chiefs of Staff should have control over shipping resources so that they could apply them to the best strategic purposes. It was hoped that something similar to the British system for the control of shipping would be set up in the United States; but the problem was more difficult since they were not a maritime nation like Great Britain, and the importance of shipping was not well realized in the United States. Many other interests clashed with strategic requirements when it came to dealing with shipping.

SIR DUDLEY POUND said that the British Chiefs of Staff had no control over the Ministry of War Transport in the matter of shipping, but they had access to all the facts and could make their case to the Prime Minister on military grounds if there was a clash of interests between strategical requirements and imports.

ADMIRAL STARK said that the United States Chiefs of Staff could not accept anything more than the first sentence of Paragraph 12, since their own organization for the control of shipping was not yet settled. It followed, therefore, that Paragraph 13 also could not be accepted at present.

SIR DUDLEY POUND undertook to let the United States Chiefs of Staff have a short memorandum on the British system for the control of shipping and raw materials.

THE CONFERENCE -

a Took note of the proposals for Post-Arcadia Collaboration made by the British Chiefs of Staff in WW-8, and of the extent to which these had been accepted by the United States Chiefs of Staff in the discussion recorded above.

b Agreed that the minute on the principle for the allocation of finished war materiel, as amended in discussion, should be submitted by the United States and British Chiefs of Staff to the President and Prime Minister respectively. (See Annex 1. Portions in Annex 1 indicated as deleted are those indicated in the discussion above as subjects for further consideration by the United States Chiefs of Staff.)

U. S. SECRET
BRITISH MOST SECRET

2. MOVEMENTS AND PROJECTS IN THE ATLANTIC THEATER - FIRST HALF OF 1942.

THE CONFERENCE had before them a report by the Joint Planning Committee on movements and projects in the Atlantic theater for the first half of 1942 (U. S. Serial ABC-4/6, British Serial WW (J.P.C.)6).

SIR DUDLEY POUND welcomed the idea of United States forces being sent to the Freetown-Bathurst area in certain circumstances, as proposed in Paragraph 14.

ADMIRAL KING pointed out that the adverse effects on other operations of carrying out various projects had only been set out in the case of North Africa. It should be made clear that any of these projects would have repercussions on others. Some reference should also be made in the final paragraph to the Northeast Brazil project.

THE CONFERENCE -

Approved the report by the Joint Planning Committee, subject to the following amendments:

a   At the end of paragraph 6, add:

"NOTE. If any of the other operations mentioned in this paper are undertaken, they will adversely affect other operations in some or all of the above ways to a greater or less extent".

b   Paragraph 17, insert new subparagraph (4) as follows:

"(4) That the United States plans for the security of Northeast Brazil should be kept active".

Renumber existing subparagraph (4) as subparagraph (5).

(See Annex 2.)

3. OPERATION SUPER-GYMNAST.

THE CONFERENCE agreed to postpone consideration of the Joint Planning Committee's reports on Super-Gymnast (U. S. ABC-4/2 and 4/2A and British WW (J.P.C.)2 and 2A) until the next meeting.

ENCLOSURES
    Annex 1 - Post-Arcadia Collaboration, WW-8 with Minute Submitted by British Chiefs of Staff Attached.
    Annex 2 - Movements and Projects in the Atlantic Theater (U.S. ABC-4/6, British WW-14).

U. S. SECRET
BRITISH MOST SECRET

BRITISH SERIAL WW-8   January 8, 1942

ANNEX 1
to
JCCSs-11

WASHINGTON WAR CONFERENCE

POST-ARCADIA COLLABORATION

MEMORANDUM BY THE BRITISH CHIEFS OF STAFF

IT IS REQUESTED THAT SPECIAL CARE SHOULD BE TAKEN TO ENSURE THE SECRECY OF THIS DOCUMENT

U. S. SECRET
BRITISH MOST SECRET

WW-8

ANNEX 1
to
JCCSs-11

January 8, 1942.

WASHINGTON WAR CONFERENCE

POST-ARCADIA COLLABORATION

MEMORANDUM BY THE BRITISH CHIEFS OF STAFF

1. We think that the United States Chiefs of Staff will wish to know what representatives of the Minister of Defence and the British Chiefs of Staff organisation it is proposed to leave in Washington after the departure of the Arcadia party.

2. To avoid confusion we suggest that hereafter the word "Joint" should be applied to Inter-Service collaboration of one Nation and the word "Combined" to collaboration between two or more ~~Allies~~ United Nations.

REPRESENTATIVE OF THE MINISTER OF DEFENCE.

3. Field Marshal Sir John Dill is remaining in Washington as representative of the Minister of Defence. He will have contacts with such authorities on the highest level as may be arranged between the President and the Prime Minister.

REPRESENTATIVES OF THE BRITISH CHIEFS OF STAFF.

4. The Heads of the Joint Staff Mission, Admiral Sir Charles Little, General Sir Colville Wemyss, and Air Marshal A. T. Harris, will continue to represent the British Chiefs of Staff in Washington. It is hoped that a meeting between the United States Chiefs of Staff or their representatives and the representatives of the British Chiefs of Staff may be held weekly or more often if necessary. An agenda would be circulated before each meeting.

U. S. SECRET
BRITISH MOST SECRET

COMBINED PLANNING.

5. For the time being, the British representatives on the Planning Staff will be -

Navy

Captain C. E. Lambe

Army

Lieut. Colonel G. F. Bourne

R. A. F.

Group Captain S. C. Strafford

COMBINED INTELLIGENCE.

6. The arrangements for production of complete intelligence to serve the Planning Staffs are of great importance and we suggest that this matter should ~~either~~ be referred to the Combined Planning Staffs for report ~~or considered by the Combined Chiefs of Staff at their next meeting~~.

7. We have here representatives of the Joint Intelligence Committee in London, and these are available to work in conjunction with any organisation the United States Chiefs of Staff may desire.

PRIORITIES AND ALLOCATION.

8. In our view the Combined Chiefs of Staff should settle the broad programme of requirements based on strategic policy. ~~We suggest that it will be the duty of the Combined Planning Staffs, advised by appropriate Allocation Officers, to watch on behalf of the Combined Chiefs of Staff the production programmes and to bring to notice instances where output does not conform to strategic policy.~~

9. ~~Similarly the Combined Chiefs of Staff should from time to time issue general directives laying down policy to govern the distribution of available weapons of war. Effect should be given to these directives by appropriate Combined Allocation Committees. These would meet periodically and make both long-term allocations (on which planning and training of forces must be based), and short-term allocations to meet immediate military needs.~~

~~10.~~ ~~The British representatives on the appropriate Combined Allocation Committees will for the present be -~~

- 2 -

U. S. SECRET
BRITISH MOST SECRET

<u>Navy</u>

~~Rear Admiral J. W. S. Dorling~~

<u>Army</u>

~~Brigadier D. Campion~~

<u>R. A. F.</u>

~~Air Commodore E. B. G. Betts~~

~~11. Allocation should be made as between the United States and the British Commonwealth, each caring for the needs of the Allies for whom it has accepted responsibility.~~

MILITARY MOVEMENTS.

12. The Combined Chiefs of Staff should settle the broad issues of priority of overseas movement. ~~In order to advise the Combined Chiefs of Staff and to coordinate the movement of United States and British troops and equipment so that the shipping resources of both countries are put to the best use, it appears to us that a Combined Body is desirable. The British representatives for such a body are available under Brigadier R. Kerr.~~

~~13. It is suggested that this Combined Body should work in close touch with the Combined Planning Staffs through whom their advice to the Combined Chiefs of Staff would be submitted.~~

SECRETARIAT.

14. A British Secretariat under Brigadier Dykes is available to serve the above organisations and to work in any similar Secretariat system which the United States Chiefs of Staff may establish.

                        (Signed)   DUDLEY POUND,

                           "   J. G. DILL,

                           "   A. T. HARRIS,
                                       (for Chief of Air Staff).

Washington, D. C.,

    January 8, 1942.

U. S. SECRET
BRITISH MOST SECRET

DRAFT MINUTE FOR SUBMISSION BY THE UNITED STATES CHIEFS

OF STAFF TO THE PRESIDENT AND BY THE BRITISH

CHIEFS OF STAFF TO THE PRIME MINISTER

"We, the combined United States - British Chiefs of Staff are agreed in principle that finished war equipment shall be allocated in accordance with strategical needs. We accordingly submit that an appropriate body should be set up, under the authority of the combined Chiefs of Staff, in Washington, and a corresponding body in London, for the purpose of giving effect to this principle."

U. S. SECRET
BRITISH MOST SECRET

U. S. ABC-4/6   January 13, 1942
BRITISH WW-14

ANNEX 2
to
JCCSs-11

UNITED STATES - BRITISH

CHIEFS OF STAFF

APPROVED AS AMENDED

REPORT BY THE UNITED STATES - BRITISH

JOINT PLANNING COMMITTEE

U. S. SERIAL ABC-4/6,   BRITISH SERIAL WW (J.P.C.) 6

MOVEMENTS AND PROJECTS IN THE ATLANTIC THEATER -

FIRST HALF OF 1942

U. S. SECRET
BRITISH MOST SECRET

January 13, 1942

U. S. ABC-4/6
BRITISH WW-14

JOINT PLANNING COMMITTEE REPORT

MOVEMENTS AND PROJECTS IN THE ATLANTIC

THEATER - FOR FIRST HALF OF 1942

1. We have carried out a study of the relative importance and interrelation of the various military movements and projects which affect the Atlantic Theater and which may be required to give effect to the agreed Grand Strategy during the first part of 1942, and submit our conclusions below.

MOVEMENTS AND RELIEFS.

ICELAND AND IRELAND

2. We consider that the move of the United States forces into Northern Ireland and the relief of the British Iceland garrison should proceed as expeditiously as possible in order to relieve British Divisions for the replacement of Australian Divisions in the Middle East and to release forces for operations in French North Africa.

3. The movement of United States Army Air Forces to the United Kingdom should proceed as soon as these forces and shipping become available, so as to increase the weight of attack on Germany.

RELIEF OF ARUBA AND CURACAO

4. The relief of Aruba and Curacao, subject to Dutch concurrence, is to be completed before the end of January.

JOINT UNITED STATES - BRITISH OCCUPATION OF FRENCH NORTH AFRICA.

5. We regard this project as of the first strategical importance in the Atlantic area. We do not, however, possess the resources within the period under consideration to force an entry into French North Africa. We cannot, therefore, initiate this operation unless we are reasonably sure of the assumptions upon which the plan is based, which are:

U. S. SECRET
BRITISH MOST SECRET

      <u>a</u> That, due to Spanish resistance, the Germans will require a period of three months before they can mount a land attack from Spain against Morocco;

      <u>b</u> That once the Spanish mainland has been invaded by Germany, our forces will be admitted freely to Spanish Morocco, and that the Spanish there will not attack us; and

      <u>c</u> That French forces will offer only sporadic resistance, if any.

During the period in which we await this opportunity we think that plans and preparations should be completed and that the movements referred to above (Paragraphs 2, 3, 4) should continue.

  6. If we undertake the North Africa operation, it will have the following adverse effects on other projects:

      <u>a</u> Reduction in British troop movements to the Middle East and Far East by 25,000 men.

      <u>b</u> Suspension of major operations against the Canaries, Cape Verdes, and Diego Suarez.

      <u>c</u> Suspension of the relief of British troops in Iceland by United States troops.

      <u>d</u> Reduction in the rate of movement of United States troops to North Ireland.

      <u>e</u> Weakening of British strength in the United Kingdom.

      <u>f</u> Inability to move sizable forces to Northeast Brazil if such action should become necessary.

      <u>g</u> Reduction in the supply of British fighter aircraft to Russia.

      <u>h</u> Serious delay in the despatch of urgently needed United States reinforcements and supplies to Pacific island positions and the Far East, to the Pacific Fleet, and to the outlying island bases.

      <u>i</u> Reduction in Atlantic convoys to the United Kingdom and Russia, due to diversions of shipping and escorts.

    (NOTE: If any of the other operations mentioned in this paper are undertaken, they will adversely affect other operations in some or all of the above ways to a greater or less extent).

U. S. SECRET
BRITISH MOST SECRET

CANARIES AND PORTUGUESE ATLANTIC ISLANDS.

7. A German invasion of Spain will lead to the immediate denial of Gibraltar as a Naval Base and in all probability the involvement of Portugal as well as Spain in the war. In those circumstances, it will be essential to secure the Canaries as a Naval Base. It is possible that the Spaniards would themselves offer us facilities in these islands. On the other hand, the Spaniards may oppose our occupation of the Canaries. While a Spanish offer of facilities would eliminate the need for a large occupying force, it would be necessary to provide sufficient additional air and anti-aircraft defenses to meet the threat of German air forces based on the mainland of Africa, as well as harbor protection for the Naval Base, and for an air patrol of the sea.

8. If we have gained an entry into French North Africa and the Spaniards subsequently acquiesce in a German move into Spain, we could not at the same time undertake an operation to capture the Canaries.

9. If the opportunity to carry out North Africa operations does not occur, and the Germans move into Spain with Spanish acquiescence, the capture of the Canaries, even against opposition, and the occupation of the Azores and Cape Verdes will become essential.

10. It has been agreed that the responsibility for the occupation of the Canaries is a British one, but it would probably be necessary to obtain Naval assistance from the United States. A British assaulting force is already earmarked for this operation and should, we consider, be kept in being.

11. Occupation of the Cape Verdes has been accepted as a United States responsibility. A portion of the United States Army forces set up for North Africa would be used for this operation. The necessary naval support would have to be provided by United States Naval Forces.

12. In the event of a German move into the Iberian Peninsula, it is almost certain that Portugal will admit British forces into the Azores, and probably Madeira. For the security of these islands the chief requirement will be air and anti-aircraft defenses and harbor protection. The provision of these forces is a British responsibility and the necessary forces should be earmarked. Considerable difficulty, however, will be found in providing the shipping for this operation simultaneously with that for North Africa or the Canaries.

13. If the move of British forces to the Azores becomes possible, we are of the opinion that the United States should occupy the Cape Verdes in order to make certain that these islands are denied to the enemy and secured for future use. The occupation of the Cape Verdes will be of considerable

U. S. SECRET
BRITISH MOST SECRET

importance if we do not succeed in gaining entry into French North Africa and are compelled to undertake operations in French West Africa at a later date.

OCCUPATION OF FRENCH WEST AFRICA

14. If we fail to occupy North Africa and Axis occupation appears imminent, then the capture of French West Africa will be essential. If we do not obtain French cooperation in French North Africa, it is unlikely that we shall gain free entry into Dakar. It is therefore necessary to plan the capture of Dakar against opposition. With the joint resources available it is not, in our opinion, possible to undertake an operation of this nature until the late Autumn of 1942 when the weather conditions become favorable. It has been agreed that the United States should be responsible for this operation and we suggest that the planning and training should be put in hand. We propose for consideration that as a preliminary, and simultaneously with the occupation of the Cape Verdes, United States Air and other appropriate forces should be moved to the Freetown - Bathurst area. Their presence in this area will increase the security of the Trans-African Reinforcement Route and the naval base at Freetown.

NORTHEAST BRAZIL

15. The security of Northeast Brazil is of strategic importance as a link in the communications between America and the Trans-African reinforcement route. Germany established in West Africa immediately becomes a threat to the South American Continent, in addition to the threat to Atlantic sea communications. The danger of an Axis-inspired uprising in Brazil, which would interrupt the air route through Africa to the Middle and Far East cannot be disregarded. The operation is a United States responsibility. Plans have been prepared and formations set up for this task.

DIEGO SUAREZ

16. Although the denial of the naval base of Diego Suarez to the enemy is of considerable strategic importance, no British force will be available to undertake this operation within the period under consideration if the force for the Canaries operation is kept in being. Moreover, if this operation were carried out in the near future it might prejudice our chance of obtaining French collaboration in North Africa. We are therefore of the opinion that we can not hold a force ready to undertake this operation at present.

17. We therefore recommend that:

    a The movement of United States Army and Air forces to Iceland, Ireland, and the United Kingdom should proceed as expeditiously as possible.

U. S. SECRET
BRITISH MOST SECRET

  <u>b</u>. That the perfection of a Joint United States - British Plan and preparations for operations in French North Africa should proceed as rapidly as possible.

  <u>c</u>. That under the hypotheses set out in this paper, the United States should prepare plans for:

   (1) The occupation of the Cape Verde Islands both against opposition and by invitation.

   (2) The capture of Dakar against opposition for the Autumn of 1942.

  <u>d</u>. That the United States plan for the security of Northeast Brazil should be kept active.

  <u>e</u>. That under the hypotheses set out in this paper, the British should prepare or perfect plans for:

   (1) The capture of the Canaries.

   (2) The occupation of the Canaries by invitation.

   (3) The occupation of the Azores and Madeira by invitation.

   (4) The capture of Diego Suarez against opposition.

U. S. SECRET
BRITISH MOST SECRET

ABC-4
JCCSs-12

January 14, 1942

CHIEFS OF STAFF CONFERENCE

FEDERAL RESERVE BUILDING

WASHINGTON, D. C.

3:00 P.M., JANUARY 14, 1942

Present

British Officers

    Navy

        Admiral of the Fleet, Sir Dudley Pound, First Sea Lord and Chief of Naval Staff
        Admiral Sir Charles Little, Joint Staff Mission

    Army

        Field Marshal Sir John Dill
        Lt. General Sir Colville Wemyss, Joint Staff Mission
        Brigadier C. S. Napier
        Lt. Colonel G. K. Bourne

    Air Force

        Air Chief Marshal Sir Charles Portal, Chief of the Air Staff
        Air Marshal A. T. Harris, Joint Staff Mission

United States Officers

    Navy

        Admiral H. R. Stark, Chief of Naval Operations
        Admiral E. J. King, Commander-in-Chief, U. S. Fleet
        Rear Admiral W. R. Sexton, President, General Board
        Rear Admiral F. J. Horne, Assistant Chief of Naval Operations
        Rear Admiral J. H. Towers, Chief of Bureau of Aeronautics
        Rear Admiral R. K. Turner, Director, War Plans Division
        Major General Thomas Holcomb, Commandant, U.S.M.C.
        Lt. Commander R. E. Libby, U.S.N.

U. S. SECRET
BRITISH MOST SECRET

    Army

        General George C. Marshall, Commanding General of the Field Forces
            and Chief of Staff
        Lt. General H. H. Arnold, Chief of the Army Air Forces and Deputy
            Chief of Staff
        Brig. General L. T. Gerow, Chief, War Plans Division
        Brig. General Brehon B. Somervell, Chief, G-4, W.D.G.S.

Joint Secretaries

        Brig. General R. E. Lee
        Captain J. L. McCrea, Aide to Chief of Naval Operations
        Captain F. C. Denebrink, U.S.N.
        Brigadier L. C. Hollis, R.M.
        Brigadier V. Dykes
        Lt. Colonel P. M. Robinett, G-2, GHQ
        Lt. Colonel W. T. Sexton, Assistant Secretary, W.D.G.S.

    1.   MOVE OF UNITED STATES REINFORCEMENTS TO THE FAR EAST. -

        BRIGADIER NAPIER, referring to the arrangements proposed for the move of urgent United States reinforcements to the Far East, said that information had now been received from London that the QUEEN MARY would take United States troops from New York via the Cape to Australia, sailing early in February. To make up for the loss of transportation from America to Northern Ireland thereby occasioned, it was proposed to allot additional British personnel ships returning from the Middle East, to sail about February 10 for Northern Ireland. Their total carrying capacity would be about 15,000. The QUEEN ELIZABETH would sail early in February from San Francisco with United States troops for Australia, and the AQUITANIA would go into the Hawaiian run at the end of February. This program had been agreed to by General Somervell.

    2.   SUPER-GYMNAST. -

        THE CONFERENCE had before them a paper prepared by the United States Planning Staff based upon a report by the Joint Planning Staff (U.S. ABC-4/2A, British WW (J.P.C.)2A).

        This paper was discussed paragraph by paragraph, and a number of amendments agreed to.

        SIR CHARLES PORTAL asked whether more United States ships could not be provided by further sacrifices, e.g., cutting into trade.

U. S. SECRET
BRITISH MOST SECRET

       GENERAL SOMERVELL said that the whole range of United States shipping, both passenger-carrying and freight, had been reviewed and no further resources could be tapped. All passenger ships, including those on the South American lines, would be taken up. The only way of increasing the number of freight ships would be to use ships already earmarked for supplies to Russia and the Middle East.

       ADMIRAL TURNER confirmed that escorts could be provided for the last American convoy but one, shown in paragraph 9 on D-163 instead of D-178. (See Annex 1)

       THE CONFERENCE accepted the paper prepared by the United States Planning Staff, subject to the amendments agreed in discussion, as a basis on which the Combined Chiefs of Staff should inform the President and the Prime Minister regarding the time factor for Super-Gymnast. (See Annex 1)

3.   POST-ARCADIA COLLABORATION. -

       THE CONFERENCE had before them a draft prepared by the United States Chiefs of Staff on Post-Arcadia Collaboration (U.S. ABC-4/CS4).

       This draft was considered paragraph by paragraph and certain amendments agreed to.

       THE CONFERENCE approved the draft as amended in discussion and agreed that it should be submitted to the President and the Prime Minister. (See Annex 2)

ENCLOSURES:
    Annex 1 - Operation Super-Gymnast (U.S. ABC-4/2A, British WW-17).
    Annex 2 - Post-Arcadia Collaboration (U.S. ABC/CS4, British WW-16).

U. S. SECRET
BRITISH MOST SECRET

U.S. ABC-4/2A
BRITISH WW-17

January 14, 1942

ANNEX 1
to
JCCSs-12

UNITED STATES - BRITISH

CHIEFS OF STAFF

ACCEPTED AS AMENDED - JOINT PLANNING COMMITTEE REPORT,

AS A BASIS ON WHICH THE COMBINED CHIEFS OF STAFF

SHOULD INFORM THE PRESIDENT AND PRIME MINISTER

REGARDING THE TIME FACTOR FOR SUPER-GYMNAST

U.S. SERIAL ABC-4/2A,
BRITISH SERIAL WW (J.P.C.)2A

OPERATION SUPER-GYMNAST

U. S. SECRET
BRITISH MOST SECRET

U. S. SERIAL ABC-4/2A
BRITISH SERIAL WW (J.P.C.) 2A

January 13, 1942

JOINT PLANNING COMMITTEE REPORT TO CHIEFS OF STAFF

OPERATION SUPER-GYMNAST

1. The Joint United States - British Planning Committee has been advised that the President and the Prime Minister have agreed to the immediate dispatch of additional United States reinforcements from the east coast to Australia, the terms of the agreement being as follows:

   a. Approved the proposal put forward by the United States Chiefs of Staff that the United States convoy sailing on the 15th January should be reduced from 16,000 to 4,000 for Northern Ireland and from 8,000 to 2,500 for Iceland, in order to permit of the dispatch to the Far East of 21,000 troops, with aircraft and other equipment.

   b. Agreed that the remainder of the proposed shipping adjustments set out in the Annex should be referred to London for confirmation.

   c. Invited Mr. Hopkins and Lord Beaverbrook to investigate the effect of the above shipping adjustment on the delivery of United States supplies to Russia during the next three months and to coordinate the provision of shipping to make good any deficiency, it being understood that nothing must be done to interfere with the planned flow of tanks, aircraft and ammunition from the United States to the Middle East.

2. Based on the above terms of agreement, the combined Chiefs of Staff have directed the Combined Planning Committee to examine and report on the following questions:

   a. The earliest date which could be fixed for D-1 of Operation Super-Gymnast, on the assumption that the shipping adjustments approved in 1 a above are carried out and that shipping to carry United States supplies to Russia is provided in full.

   b. To what extent Operation Super-Gymnast could be executed, on the assumption that the favorable opportunity arises at some date between the end of February and the date on which D-1 of the full operation could be fixed (vide 2 a above).

U. S. SECRET
BRITISH MOST SECRET

REPLY TO THE FIRST QUESTION

BRITISH

1. The movement of United States Troops to Australia will not affect the readiness date of the British to carry out their part of Super-Gymnast.

UNITED STATES

2. The readiness of United States Troops to carry out Super-Gymnast will not be affected by the movement of reinforcements to the Far East. The delay to Super-Gymnast caused by the Far East movement will depend upon the date of return to Atlantic ports of the ships involved in that movement.

3. We estimate that the vessels diverted from the Atlantic to make the Far East move can be back in the Atlantic ports on the following dates:

    <u>a</u>. Passenger vessels ..... April 10 - 20
    <u>b</u>. Cargo vessels .... May   15 - 25

(Capacity of the above group of vessels is 22,000
    troops and 230,000 tons of cargo).

4. The execution of Super-Gymnast, as originally planned, is dependent upon the return of the Far East convoy, therefore the earliest date that could be fixed for D-1 is May 25.

5. The May 25 date can not be accepted without certain reservations, since no allowance has been made for ship losses and possible increased demands for shipping arising from enemy operations, accelerated production, and additional lend-lease commitments. Furthermore, it seems probable that these vessels may continue to be needed in the Pacific for further movements to Australia.

REPLY TO THE SECOND QUESTION

BRITISH AVAILABLE FORCES

6. British land forces, i.e., one armored division and two divisions with antiaircraft units, will be ready for dispatch. The British air contingent of Gymnast consisting of three fighter and two A.C. squadrons could also be made ready. This force is not alone sufficient, but could not be increased from British resources.

U. S. SECRET
BRITISH MOST SECRET

UNITED STATES AVAILABLE FORCES

7. United States Forces, as originally planned for Super-Gymnast, will be available, but their participation will be limited by the withdrawal of shipping for the troop movements in the Pacific. Combat loaded ships for one Division (12,000) are being held in readiness. This shipping will permit the employment of that division. It can be supported by one carrier group of naval aircraft or equivalent, disembarked from an aircraft carrier. All antiaircraft troops would have to be found by the British, also base troops, until additional United States shipping could be made available, either from Pacific or from shipping now employed on other tasks. This latter shipping is more fully discussed in Paragraph 11 below.

RATE OF MOVEMENT

8. The rate at which the British force could be received would not be limited, as in the Super-Gymnast plan, by the capacity of Casablanca Port. It would depend upon the provision of shipping and naval escorts. The following table is based upon the assumption that the British could not afford to rob the Middle and Far East reinforcements of more than 25,000 men from one reinforcement convoy. The United States program is based upon the repeated use of the combat loaded ships, and the use of no other troop transports until the return to the Atlantic Coast of the Far East cargo convoy, about 15 - 25 May. For movements after the first one, 8 additional cargo vessels will be required. Possible acceleration of the movement will be governed by the priority needs stated in Paragraph 11 below.

9. The table below shows the earliest dates on which British and United States forces can arrive at Casablanca if D-1 falls on March 1st:

		CASABLANCA		ALGIERS
March 1	D-1	BRITISH	U.S.	BRITISH
Mar. 28	D-28	5,000	12,000	7,000
	D-43	6,000 *		16,000
	D-73	22,000		
	D-88		12,000	
	D-103	22,000		
	D-118		22,000	
July 21	D-133	12,000 *		
	D-148		12,000	
	D-163		22,000	
Sept. 19	D-193		12,000	
	Totals	67,000	92,000	23,000

* See Paragraph 10.

U. S. SECRET
BRITISH MOST SECRET

ACCELERATION OF MOVEMENT

BRITISH

10. If the situation were such that we could afford to stop the flow of British reinforcements to the Middle and Far East completely for a time, the second British convoy could be increased from 6,000 to 18,000 capacity, thus eliminating the fifth British convoy shown above.

UNITED STATES

11. The priorities listed below will govern the availability of additional United States vessels for Super-Gymnast:

    1st Priority: Continuous maintenance of existing overseas Army and Navy garrisons and the United States Fleets.

    2nd Priority: Continued delivery of supplies to Russia, and planned flow of tanks, aircraft, and ammunition to the Middle East.

    3rd Priority: Continuous movements and maintenance of United States forces in the Far East.

12. All military requirements for shipping other than those listed above will have to be deferred, including:

    a. Reinforcements to Hawaii and other overseas possessions and bases.

    b. Movements to Iceland and North Ireland.

13. If this is done, we estimate that additional passenger vessels up to an estimated capacity of 12,400 might be available after about four weeks' notice.

14. Approximately 13 - 15 cargo vessels will be required in addition to the passenger vessels. The availability of the cargo ships will have to be determined by the Maritime Commission.

U. S. SECRET
BRITISH MOST SECRET

U. S. ABC-4/CS4   January 14, 1942
BRITISH WW-16

ANNEX 2
to
JCCSs-12

UNITED STATES - BRITISH

CHIEFS OF STAFF

APPROVED AS AMENDED - UNITED STATES CHIEFS OF STAFF

MEMORANDUM

POST-ARCADIA COLLABORATION

U. S. SECRET
BRITISH MOST SECRET

U. S. ABC-4/CS4　　　　　　　　　　　　　　　　　　　　January 14, 1942
BRITISH WW-16

WASHINGTON WAR CONFERENCE

POST-ARCADIA COLLABORATION

MEMORANDUM BY COMBINED CHIEFS OF STAFF

1. In order to provide for the continuance of the necessary machinery to effect collaboration between the United Nations after the departure from Washington of the British Chiefs of Staff, the Combined Chiefs of Staff (formerly designated as "Joint Chiefs of Staff") propose the broad principles and basic organization herein outlined.

2. To avoid confusion we suggest that hereafter the word "Joint" be applied to Inter-Service collaboration of ONE NATION, and the word "Combined" to collaboration between two or more of the UNITED NATIONS.

3. DEFINITIONS. -

   a. The term "Combined Chiefs of Staff" is defined as the British Chiefs of Staff (or in their absence from Washington, their duly accredited representatives), and the United States opposite numbers of the British Chiefs of Staff.

   b. The term "Combined Staff Planners" is defined as the body of officers duly appointed by the Combined Chiefs of Staff to make such studies, draft such plans, and perform such other work as may from time to time be placed on the "Combined Chiefs of Staff Agenda" by that Body, and duly delegated by them to the Combined Staff Planners.

   c. The "Combined Secretariat" is defined as the body of officers duly appointed by the Combined Chiefs of Staff to maintain necessary records, prepare and distribute essential papers, and perform such other work as is delegated to them by the Combined Chiefs of Staff.

4. PERSONNEL. -

   a. The Heads of the Joint Staff Mission, Admiral Sir Charles Little, Lt. General Sir Colville Wemyss, and Air Marshal A. T. Harris, will represent the British Chiefs of Staff in Washington.

   b. The Joint Staff Planners will be:

U. S. SECRET
BRITISH MOST SECRET

        (1)   FOR THE BRITISH (for the time being):

            Captain C. E. Lambe, R.N.
            Lt. Col. G. K. Bourne, British Army
            Group Captain S. C. Strafford, R.A.F.

        (2)   FOR THE UNITED STATES, the principal members are:

            Rear Admiral R. K. Turner, U.S. Navy
            Brig. Gen. L. T. Gerow, U.S. Army
            Capt. R. E. Davison, U.S. Navy
            Col. E. L. Naiden, U.S. Army

    c.   COMBINED SECRETARIAT

The British members of the Combined Secretariat will be headed by Brigadier Dykes. The United States members will be headed by Commander L. R. McDowell, U.S. Navy.

5.   THE COMBINED CHIEFS OF STAFF shall develop and submit recommendations as follows:

    a.   For the ABDA Area, specifically as set forth in the Directive, Annex 2 to U.S. ABC-4/5, British WW-6, dated January 5, 1942.

    b.   For other areas in which the United Nations may decide to act in concert, along the same general lines as in a above, modified as necessary to meet the particular circumstances.

6.   THE COMBINED CHIEFS OF STAFF shall accordingly:

    a.   Recommend the broad program of requirements based on strategic considerations.

    b.   Submit general directives as to the policy governing the distribution of available weapons of war. (It is agreed that finished war equipment shall be allocated in accordance with strategical needs; to effectuate this principle, we recommend the utilization of appropriate bodies in London and Washington, under the authority of the Combined Chiefs of Staff).

    c.   Settle the broad issues of priority of overseas military movements.

U. S. SECRET
BRITISH MOST SECRET

7. The question of the production and dissemination of complete Military Intelligence to serve the Combined Chiefs of Staff and Combined Staff Planners has been referred to the latter body for a report. Here also, it is contemplated that existing machinery will be largely continued.

8. It is planned that the Combined Chiefs of Staff will meet weekly, or more often if necessary; an agenda will be circulated before each meeting.

U. S. SECRET
BRITISH MOST SECRET

PART II

APPROVED DOCUMENTS

U. S. SECRET
BRITISH MOST SECRET

U. S. ABC-4/1
BRITISH WW-5   December 29, 1941

UNITED STATES - BRITISH

CHIEFS OF STAFF

APPROVED

REPORT BY THE U. S. - BRITISH JOINT
PLANNING COMMITTEE
U.S. ABC-4/1, BRITISH WW(JPC)1

PRIORITIES FOR UNITED STATES AND

UNITED KINGDOM OVERSEAS EXPEDITIONS

IN THE ATLANTIC OCEAN

U. S. SECRET
BRITISH MOST SECRET

U. S. SERIAL ABC-4/1
BRITISH SERIAL WW(J.P.C.)1

PRIORITIES FOR UNITED STATES AND UNITED KINGDOM OVERSEAS EXPEDITIONS IN THE ATLANTIC OCEAN

REPORT BY THE U. S. - BRITISH JOINT PLANNING COMMITTEE

1.   One of the directives to the Joint Planning Committee issued by the Chiefs of Staff Committee on December 24, 1941, may be summarized as follows:-

Study and report outline plans for the overseas employment of United States and British troops in the Atlantic region, indicating recommended relative priorities of importance:

   a   The relief by United States troops of British troops in Iceland and North Ireland.

   b   The occupation by invitation of the following positions:

      (1) The Azores.
      (2) The Cape Verde Islands.
      (3) The Canary Islands.
      (4) French West Africa.
      (5) French North Africa.
      (6) Diego Suarez in Madagascar.
      (7) Curacao and Aruba.
      (8) Northeast Brazil.

2.   The Joint Planning Committee recommends that the initial occupation by invitation of the foreign positions indicated in the directive should be allocated as follows:

   a   To the United States - the occupation of the Cape Verde Islands, French West Africa, Curacao and Aruba, Northeast Brazil.

   b   To the United Kingdom - the occupation of the Azores, the Canary Islands, and Diego Suarez in Madagascar.

   c   To the United States and the United Kingdom acting jointly - the occupation of French North Africa.

U. S. SECRET
BRITISH MOST SECRET

3. If the operation in French North Africa as submitted in our plan (U. S. Serial ABC-4/2, British Serial WW) is undertaken, we see no prospect of any other major movements being carried out in the Atlantic area for at least three months, and normal reinforcements to the eastward from the United Kingdom will be severely curtailed. The reason is lack of an adequate amount of troop transport, in view of the heavy reinforcements being sent to Hawaii, Samoa, and Australia, and requirements for the continuous support of outlying United States and United Kingdom field armies, garrisons, and naval forces. Furthermore, minimum requirements for naval protection of new lines of naval communications will seriously reduce the protection now being afforded the trade routes in the Atlantic and Indian Oceans.

4. No major overseas operations can be performed by the United States unless adequate shipping is immediately made available for preparation as troop transports.

U. S. SECRET
BRITISH MOST SECRET

U.S. ABC-4/2A
BRITISH WW-17

January 14, 1942

UNITED STATES - BRITISH

CHIEFS OF STAFF

ACCEPTED AS AMENDED - JOINT PLANNING COMMITTEE REPORT,

AS A BASIS ON WHICH THE COMBINED CHIEFS OF STAFF

SHOULD INFORM THE PRESIDENT AND PRIME MINISTER

REGARDING THE TIME FACTOR FOR SUPER-GYMNAST

U.S. SERIAL ABC-4/2A,
BRITISH SERIAL WW (J.P.C.)2A

OPERATION SUPER-GYMNAST

U. S. SECRET
BRITISH MOST SECRET

U. S. SERIAL ABC-4/2A
BRITISH SERIAL WW (J.P.C.) 2A

January 13, 1942

JOINT PLANNING COMMITTEE REPORT TO CHIEFS OF STAFF

OPERATION SUPER-GYMNAST

1. The Joint United States - British Planning Committee has been advised that the President and the Prime Minister have agreed to the immediate dispatch of additional United States reinforcements from the east coast to Australia, the terms of the agreement being as follows:

   a. Approved the proposal put forward by the United States Chiefs of Staff that the United States convoy sailing on the 15th January should be reduced from 16,000 to 4,000 for Northern Ireland and from 8,000 to 2,500 for Iceland, in order to permit of the dispatch to the Far East of 21,000 troops, with aircraft and other equipment.

   b. Agreed that the remainder of the proposed shipping adjustments set out in the Annex should be referred to London for confirmation.

   c. Invited Mr. Hopkins and Lord Beaverbrook to investigate the effect of the above shipping adjustment on the delivery of United States supplies to Russia during the next three months and to coordinate the provision of shipping to make good any deficiency, it being understood that nothing must be done to interfere with the planned flow of tanks, aircraft and ammunition from the United States to the Middle East.

2. Based on the above terms of agreement, the combined Chiefs of Staff have directed the Combined Planning Committee to examine and report on the following questions:

   a. The earliest date which could be fixed for D-1 of Operation Super-Gymnast, on the assumption that the shipping adjustments approved in 1 a above are carried out and that shipping to carry United States supplies to Russia is provided in full.

   b. To what extent Operation Super-Gymnast could be executed, on the assumption that the favorable opportunity arises at some date between the end of February and the date on which D-1 of the full operation could be fixed (vide 2 a above).

U. S. SECRET
BRITISH MOST SECRET

REPLY TO THE FIRST QUESTION

BRITISH

    1. The movement of United States Troops to Australia will not affect the readiness date of the British to carry out their part of Super-Gymnast.

UNITED STATES

    2. The readiness of United States Troops to carry out Super-Gymnast will not be affected by the movement of reinforcements to the Far East. The delay to Super-Gymnast caused by the Far East movement will depend upon the date of return to Atlantic ports of the ships involved in that movement.

    3. We estimate that the vessels diverted from the Atlantic to make the Far East move can be back in the Atlantic ports on the following dates:

        a. Passenger vessels ..... April 10 - 20
        b. Cargo vessels .... May   15 - 25

  (Capacity of the above group of vessels is 22,000
      troops and 230,000 tons of cargo).

    4. The execution of Super-Gymnast, as originally planned, is dependent upon the return of the Far East convoy, therefore the earliest date that could be fixed for D-1 is May 25.

    5. The May 25 date can not be accepted without certain reservations, since no allowance has been made for ship losses and possible increased demands for shipping arising from enemy operations, accelerated production, and additional lend-least commitments. Furthermore, it seems probable that these vessels may continue to be needed in the Pacific for further movements to Australia.

REPLY TO THE SECOND QUESTION

BRITISH AVAILABLE FORCES

    6. British land forces, i.e., one armored division and two divisions with antiaircraft units, will be ready for dispatch. The British air contingent of Gymnast consisting of three fighter and two A.C. squadrons could also be made ready. This force is not alone sufficient, but could not be increased from British resources.

U. S. SECRET
BRITISH MOST SECRET

UNITED STATES AVAILABLE FORCES

7. United States Forces, as originally planned for Super-Gymnast, will be available, but their participation will be limited by the withdrawal of shipping for the troop movements in the Pacific. Combat loaded ships for one Division (12,000) are being held in readiness. This shipping will permit the employment of that division. It can be supported by one carrier group of naval aircraft or equivalent, disembarked from an aircraft carrier. All antiaircraft troops would have to be found by the British, also base troops, until additional United States shipping could be made available, either from Pacific or from shipping now employed on other tasks. This latter shipping is more fully discussed in Paragraph 11 below.

RATE OF MOVEMENT

8. The rate at which the British force could be received would not be limited, as in the Super-Gymnast plan, by the capacity of Casablanca Port. It would depend upon the provision of shipping and naval escorts. The following table is based upon the assumption that the British could not afford to rob the Middle and Far East reinforcements of more than 25,000 men from one reinforcement convoy. The United States program is based upon the repeated use of the combat loaded ships, and the use of no other troop transports until the return to the Atlantic Coast of the Far East cargo convoy, about 15 - 25 May. For movements after the first one, 8 additional cargo vessels will be required. Possible acceleration of the movement will be governed by the priority needs stated in Paragraph 11 below.

9. The table below shows the earliest dates on which British and United States forces can arrive at Casablanca if D-1 falls on March 1st:

		CASABLANCA		ALGIERS
March 1	D-1	BRITISH	U.S.	BRITISH
Mar. 28	D-28	5,000	12,000	7,000
	D-43	6,000 *		16,000
	D-73	22,000		
	D-88		12,000	
	D-103	22,000		
	D-118		22,000	
July 21	D-133	12,000 *		
	D-148		12,000	
	D-163		22,000	
Sept. 19	D-193		12,000	
	Totals	67,000	92,000	23,000

* See Paragraph 10.

U. S. SECRET
BRITISH MOST SECRET

ACCELERATION OF MOVEMENT

BRITISH

10. If the situation were such that we could afford to stop the flow of British reinforcements to the Middle and Far East completely for a time, the second British convoy could be increased from 6,000 to 18,000 capacity, thus eliminating the fifth British convoy shown above.

UNITED STATES

11. The priorities listed below will govern the availability of additional United States vessels for Super-Gymnast:

    1st Priority: Continuous maintenance of existing overseas Army and Navy garrisons and the United States Fleets.

    2nd Priority: Continued delivery of supplies to Russia, and planned flow of tanks, aircraft, and ammunition to the Middle East.

    3rd Priority: Continuous movements and maintenance of United States forces in the Far East.

12. All military requirements for shipping other than those listed above will have to be deferred, including:

    a. Reinforcements to Hawaii and other overseas possessions and bases.

    b. Movements to Iceland and North Ireland.

13. If this is done, we estimate that additional passenger vessels up to an estimated capacity of 12,400 might be available after about four weeks' notice.

14. Approximately 13 - 15 cargo vessels will be required in addition to the passenger vessels. The availability of the cargo ships will have to be determined by the Maritime Commission.

U.S. ABC-4/3
BRITISH WW-4

December 31, 1941

REPORT

By

UNITED STATES - BRITISH

CHIEFS OF STAFF

SUPPORTING MEASURES FOR THE SOUTHWEST PACIFIC

(THE FAR EAST AREA AND ADJACENT REGIONS)

UNTIL ESTABLISHMENT OF UNIFIED COMMAND.

Downgraded to *paper (l GM 143-58 dated 6-25-58*
U.S. UNCLASSIFIED *British Classification retained*

U. S. SECRET
BRITISH MOST SECRET

U.S. ABC-4/3　　　　　　　　　　　　　　　　　　　　December 31, 1941
BRITISH WW(J.P.C.)3

      The United States and British Chiefs of Staff approved the Joint Planning Committee report of December 29, 1941, on "Supporting Measures for the Southwest Pacific" as appropriate action to be taken in the interim prior to the establishment of the unified command of the forces in that region.

      The United States and British Chiefs of Staff agreed to send immediately to the United States and British Commanders-in-Chief in the Far East Area the following telegram:

      "The general strategic policy for operations in the Far Eastern theatre which has been agreed upon by the United States and British Chiefs of Staff is as follows:-

      <u>a</u>. To hold the Malay Barrier, defined as the line Malay Peninsula, Sumatra, Java, and North Australia, as the basic defensive position in that theatre and to operate sea, land, and air forces in as great depth as possible forward of the Barrier in order to oppose the Japanese southward advance.

      <u>b</u>. To hold Burma and Australia as essential supporting positions for the theatre, and Burma as essential to the support of China, and to the defense of India.

      <u>c</u>. To reestablish communications through the Dutch East Indies with Luzon and to support the Philippines' Garrison.

      <u>d</u>. To maintain essential communications within the theatre.

      In disposing of the reinforcements arriving in that theatre, you should be guided by the above policy and consider the needs of the theatre as a whole. To this end, close co-operation among the British, Dutch and United States Commanders is essential, and you should continue to concert measures accordingly.

      The British Commander-in-Chief, Far East, will inform the Dutch and request their cooperation."

TELEGRAM

U. S. SECRET
BRITISH MOST SECRET

U.S. SERIAL ABC-4/3
BRITISH SERIAL WW(J.P.C.) 3.

December 28, 1941

JOINT PLANNING COMMITTEE REPORT

TO

CHIEFS OF STAFF

SUPPORTING MEASURES FOR THE SOUTHWEST PACIFIC

(THE FAR EAST AREA AND ADJACENT REGIONS)

DIRECTIVE

    1.   CHIEFS OF STAFF DIRECTIVE TO THE JOINT PLANNING COMMITTEE.

Until such time as the wider problem of the unified control of all available forces in the Southwest Pacific Area is solved, the aim must be to reinforce the Philippine Islands, Malaya, and the Netherlands East Indies, to the maximum extent, and to make the best possible arrangements for ensuring the safe arrival and the most effective intervention of these reinforcements.

Having regard to the existing situation in the Far East and the Southwest Pacific, the Joint Planning Committee is asked to make recommendations as to the disposition of the reinforcements, particularly air forces, expected to be available in the Southwest Pacific Area on:-

        a. 15th January, 1942.

        b. 1st February, 1942.

on the following alternative assumptions:-

        (1) The Philippines and Singapore both hold.

        (2) Singapore and the Netherlands East Indies hold, but the Philippines do not.

        (3) Neither Singapore nor the Philippines holds.

CONCEPT OF OPERATIONS

    2.   Our basic strategic concept is to maintain initially the strategic defensive in the Southwest Pacific Theatre. The present strength

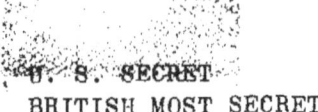

U. S. SECRET
BRITISH MOST SECRET

of forces in that area is insufficient to maintain that defensive position.

After providing immediate reinforcements for defense, and as additional forces become available, it will become possible to undertake offensive operations and ultimately to conduct an all-out offensive against Japan. Accordingly, although our operations in the near future must be primarily for defense, they should be so conducted as to further our preparations for a future offensive.

3. The general strategic policy should therefore be:-

a. To hold the Malay Barrier, defined as the line Malay Peninsula, Sumatra, Java, North Australia, as the basic defensive position of the Far East Area, and to operate air and sea forces in as great depth as possible forward of the Barrier in order to oppose the Japanese southward advance.

b. To hold Burma and Australia as essential supporting positions for the Far East Area, and Burma as essential to the support of China and to the defense of India.

c. To reestablish communications with Luzon and to support the Philippines' Garrison.

d. To maintain communications to Burma and Australia, and to and within the Far East Area.

e. To obtain in the Far East Area and Australasia all possible supplies to relieve shipping requirements.

FORCES AND REINFORCEMENTS

4. The estimated strength of forces initially in the Area, and the reinforcements ordered or planned to be sent are shown in the attached tables (Annexes I, II, and III). Future reinforcements should be planned in accordance with approved strategic policy, having due regard to the essential requirements of other theatres.

RECOMMENDATIONS

5. It is recommended that, until such time as the wider problem of the unified control of all available forces in the Southwest Pacific Area is solved:-

BRITISH MOST SECRET

    a. Under the assumption that the Philippines and Singapore both hold, the total reinforcements available up to 1st February, 1942, as shown on the attached table, should go forward as now arranged, subject to the direction of the commander to whom they are assigned.

    b. Under the assumption that Singapore and the Netherlands East Indies hold, but the Philippines do not, the total United States reinforcements available up to 1st February, 1942, should be employed in furtherance of the defenses of key points on the Malay Barrier, and for protection of the vital lines of communication from the east. In the absence of unity of command, detailed dispositions of these reinforcements must be left to the senior United States Army commander, in collaboration with the senior British, Dutch, and Australian commanders. Under this assumption the planned disposition of British reinforcements remains unchanged.

    c. Under the assumption that neither Singapore nor the Philippines holds, the total reinforcements available up to 1st February, 1942, be used for the defense of the remainder of the Malay Barrier, Burma, and Australia, United States reinforcements being used to the eastward, and British reinforcements to the westward.

NOTE:- The subject of reinforcements for New Zealand and Fiji is being considered separately.

BRITISH MOST SECRET

FAR EAST FORCES AND REINFORCEMENTS THEREFOR

UNITED STATES

FORCES NOW IN THE FAR EAST	DUE IN FAR EAST BY JANUARY 15, 1942	DUE IN FAR EAST BETWEEN JAN. 15 AND FEBRUARY 1	TENTATIVELY PLANNED OR UNDER ORDER FOR FAR EAST
(a) <u>Naval</u>	(a) <u>Naval</u>	(a) <u>Naval</u>	(a) <u>Naval</u>
2 Cruisers 13 Destroyers (3 damaged) 27 Submarines (less losses) 7 Patrol Bombers	12 Patrol Bombers	None	None
(b) <u>Army</u>	(b) <u>Army</u>	(b) <u>Army</u>	(b) <u>Army</u>
<u>Philippines</u> (<u>Luzon</u>) 40,000 as of December 22, 1941. <u>Australia</u> 2 Regts. Field Artillery Service Troops	Small Arms Ammunition Artillery Ammunition AA Ammunition Gasoline	None	Supplies & Gasoline
(c) <u>Air</u>	(c) <u>Air</u>	(c) <u>Air</u>	(c) <u>Air</u>
<u>Philippines (Dec. 25)</u> Few Pursuit planes for reconnaissance <u>Australia</u> 18 Pursuit planes 52 Dive bombers 11 Heavy Bombers	55 Pursuit 23 Heavy Bombers	67 Pursuit 57 Heavy Bombers	To make total of: 4 Gps. Pursuit (320) 2 Gps. Heavy Bombers (70) 2 Gps Medium Bombers (114) 1 Gp. Light Bombers (57) (plus certain reserves)

ANNEX I

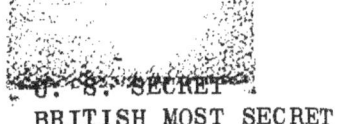
BRITISH MOST SECRET

FAR EAST FORCES AND REINFORCEMENTS THEREFOR
BRITISH COMMONWEALTH

FORCES IN THE FAR EAST ON DECEMBER 7, 1941	DUE IN FAR EAST BY JANUARY 15, 1942	DUE IN FAR EAST BETWEEN JANUARY 15 AND FEBRUARY 1	TENTATIVELY PLANNED OR UNDER ORDER FOR FAR EAST
(a) <u>Naval</u> 2 Cruisers 8 Destroyers	(a) <u>Naval</u> 5 Additional Escort Vessels	(a) <u>Naval</u> 2 Submarines	(a) <u>Naval</u> None
(b) <u>Army</u> 9 and 11 Ind. Divs.) 8 Aus. Div.) Malaya (less one Bde.) One Div. (Burma) 2 Inf. Bdes. (Singapore)	(b) <u>Army</u> (to Malaya) One Bde. Gp. 17 Ind. Div. One Bde. Gp. 18 Div. One AA Regt. (light) One AA Regt. (heavy) One Antitank Regt.	(b) <u>Army</u> (to Malaya) One Bde. Gp. 17 Ind. Div. One Bde. Gp. 18 Div. Drafts for 9 and 11 Ind. Divs. One Sq. Light Tanks.	(b) <u>Army</u> (Malaya) Two AA Regts. (light) One AA Regt. (heavy) One Bde. Gp. 14 Ind. Div. 18 Div. (less two Bde. Gps). <u>To Burma</u> 14 Ind. Div. (less one Bde. Gp.) One Bde. Gp. 17th Ind. Div. 5th or 34th Ind. Div.
(c) <u>Air</u> <u>Malaya</u> 2 Bomber Sqns. 2 Bomber Recce Sqns. 6 Fighter Sqns 2 T.B. Sqns. 1 G.R. Flying Boat Sqn.	(c) <u>Air</u> <u>Malaya</u> 4 PBY's 1 Fighter Sq. (51 Hurricanes) 1 Bomber Sq. (Blenheims) 1 Bomber Recce (Hudsons)	(c) <u>Air</u> <u>Malaya</u> 2 Fighter Sqns. (48 Hurricanes)	(c) <u>Air</u> Plans not complete
<u>Burma</u> ½ Bomber Sqn. ½ Fighter Sqn.	<u>Burma</u> None	<u>Burma</u> 1 Fighter Sqn. (Hurricanes)	

ANNEX II

BRITISH MOST SECRET

AUSTRALIA

Forces now in the Far East

(a) <u>Naval</u>

    2 Heavy Cruisers
    2 Light Cruisers
    4 Destroyers

(b) <u>Army</u>

    1 Brig Gp. of 8th
       Australian Div.
    5 Divisions (Infantry)
    2 Divisions (Cavalry)
    1 Division (Armored)
      (Not as yet equipped)

(c) <u>Air</u>

    160 First line planes
    300 - 400 Training planes
  15,000 Air officers and men
  40,000 In Training

DUTCH

Forces now in the Far East

(a) <u>Naval</u>

    4 Cruisers
    7 Destroyers
   15 Submarines
  2 - 3 Submarines (Expected)
             (Later)

(b) <u>Army</u>

    3 Div's Java
    7 Bn's Sumatra
    4 Bn's Borneo
    1 Bn Celebes
    1 Bn Timor
    1 Bn Moluccas

(c) <u>Air</u>

    6 Bomber Sqns.
    4 Fighter Sqns.
  108 Navy Aircraft
   40 Patrol Planes

ANNEX III

U. S. SECRET
BRITISH MOST SECRET

U. S. SERIAL   ABC-4/4 (FINAL)   December 31, 1941
BRITISH SERIAL   WW(J.P.C.)4

UNITED STATES - BRITISH

CHIEFS OF STAFF

APPROVED

PROPOSED TASKS FOR THE JOINT PLANNING

COMMITTEE

U. S. SECRET
BRITISH MOST SECRET

U.S. SERIAL ABC-4/4 (FINAL)　　　　　　　　　　　　　　　December 31, 1941
BRITISH SERIAL WW(J.P.C.)4

PROPOSED TASKS FOR THE JOINT PLANNING COMMITTEE

1. A study of the relative importance and interrelation of the various military projects and movements which affect the Atlantic theatre and which may be required to give effect to the agreed Grand Strategy during the first part of 1942.

    This report will include consideration of the following:

    a. MOVEMENTS

        (1) Relief of Iceland.

        (2) Movement of three Divisions and one Armored Division from the United States to Northern Ireland.

        (3) Movement of United States air forces to the United Kingdom.

        (4) Relief of British in Aruba and Curacao.

    b. PROJECTS

        (1) Joint United States-British occupation of French North Africa.

        (2) United States occupation of:

            (a) French West Africa and Cape Verde Islands.

            (b) Northeast Brazil.

        (3) British occupation of:

            (a) The Azores.

            (b) The Canaries and Madeira.

            (c) Diego Suarez.

2. Coordination of the Victory Programs of the United States and the British Commonwealth and adjustment of their broad outlines in accordance with strategic considerations and production possibilities.

U. S. SECRET
BRITISH MOST SECRET

    3. A consideration of any steps that should be taken in the light of experience up to date to implement, improve, or extend the system of collaboration between the United States-British Staffs as laid down in ABC-1; the need for allocating joint resources on a strategic basis to be taken into account.

> NOTE: Consideration of the Southwest Pacific Theatre, including the matter of unity of command therein, was treated as a first priority and a decision reached prior to the acceptance of the foregoing document.

U. S. SECRET
BRITISH MOST SECRET

U.S. ABC-4/5
BRITISH WW-6 (APPROVED)
(SUPERSEDES ABC-4/5, WW-3 FINAL)   January 10, 1942.

REPORT

BY

UNITED STATES - BRITISH

CHIEFS OF STAFF

DIRECTIVE TO THE SUPREME

COMMANDER IN THE ABDA AREA

APPROVED BY THE PRESIDENT AND THE PRIME MINISTER

U. S. SECRET
BRITISH MOST SECRET

U. S. SERIAL ABC-4/5 (APPROVED)
BRITISH SERIAL WW-6
SUPERSEDES ABC-4/5, BRITISH WW-3 (FINAL)

January 10, 1942.

DIRECTIVE TO THE SUPREME COMMANDER IN THE ABDA AREA

BY AGREEMENT AMONG THE GOVERNMENTS OF

AUSTRALIA, THE NETHERLANDS, THE UNITED

KINGDOM, AND THE UNITED STATES, HEREINAFTER

REFERRED TO AS THE ABDA GOVERNMENTS:

1. AREA.-

A strategic area has been constituted, to comprise initially all land and sea areas included in the general region Burma - Malaya - Netherlands East Indies and the Philippines; more precisely defined in Annex 1. This area will be known as the ABDA Area.

2. FORCES.-

You have been designated as the Supreme Commander of the ABDA Area and of all armed forces, afloat, ashore, and in the air, of the ABDA Governments which are or will be:-

    a. Stationed in the Area;

    b. Located in Australian territory when such forces have been allotted by the respective governments for services in or in support of the ABDA Area

You are not authorized to transfer from the territory of any of the ABDA Governments land forces of that government without the consent of the local commander or his government.

3. The Deputy Supreme Commander and, if required, a commander of the combined naval forces and a commander of the combined air forces will be jointly designated by the ABDA Governments.

4. No government will materially reduce its armed forces assigned to your Area nor any commitments made by it for reinforcing its forces in your Area except after giving to the other governments, and to you, timely information pertaining thereto.

U. S. SECRET
BRITISH MOST SECRET

5. STRATEGIC CONCEPT AND POLICY.-

The basic strategic concept of the ABDA Governments for the conduct of the war in your Area is not only in the immediate future to maintain as many key positions as possible, but to take the offensive at the earliest opportunity and ultimately to conduct an all-out offensive against Japan. The first essential is to gain general air superiority at the earliest possible moment, through the employment of concentrated air power. The piecemeal employment of air forces should be minimized. Your operations should be so conducted as to further preparations for the offensive.

6. THE GENERAL STRATEGIC POLICY WILL THEREFORE BE:-

　　a. To hold the Malay Barrier, defined as the line Malay Peninsula, Sumatra, Java, North Australia, as the basic defensive position of the ABDA Area, and to operate sea, land, and air forces in as great depth as possible forward of the Barrier in order to oppose the Japanese southward advance.

　　b. To hold Burma and Australia as essential supporting positions for the Area, and Burma as essential to the support of China, and to the defense of India.

　　c. To reestablish communications through the Dutch East Indies with Luzon and to support the Philippines' Garrison.

　　d. To maintain essential communications within the Area.

7. DUTIES, RESPONSIBILITIES, AND AUTHORITY OF THE SUPREME COMMANDER.-

You will coordinate in the ABDA Area the strategic operations of all armed forces of the ABDA Governments; assign them strategic missions and objectives; where desirable, arrange for the formation of task forces, whether national or international, for the execution of specific operations; and appoint any officer, irrespective of seniority or nationality, to command such task forces.

8. While you will have no responsibilities in respect of the internal administration of the respective forces under your command, you are authorized to direct and coordinate the creation and development of administrative facilities and the broad allocation of war materials.

9. You will dispose reinforcements which from time to time may be dispatched to the Area by the ABDA Governments.

10. You are authorized to require from the Commanders of the armed forces under your command such reports as you deem necessary in the discharge of your responsibilities as Supreme Commander.

U. S. SECRET
BRITISH MOST SECRET

11. You are authorized to control the issue of all communiques concerning the forces under your command.

12. Through the channels specified in Paragraph 18, you may submit recommendations to the ABDA Governments on any matters pertaining to the furtherance of your mission.

13. LIMITATIONS.-

Your authority and control with respect to the various portions of the ABDA Area and to the forces assigned thereto will normally be exercised through the commanders duly appointed by their respective governments. Interference is to be avoided in the administrative processes of the armed forces of any of the ABDA Governments, including free communication between them and their respective governments. No alteration or revision is to be made in the basic tactical organization of such forces, and each national component of a task force will normally operate under its own commander and will not be subdivided into small units for attachment to the other national components of the task force, except in the case of urgent necessity. In general, your instructions and orders will be limited to those necessary for effective coordination of forces in the execution of your mission.

14. RELATIONS WITH ABDA GOVERNMENTS.-

The ABDA Governments will jointly and severally support you in the execution of the duties and responsibilities as herein defined, and in the exercise of the authority herein delegated and limited. Commanders of all sea, land, and air forces within your Area will be immediately informed by their respective governments that, from a date to be notified, all orders and instructions issued by you in conformity with the provisions of this directive will be considered by such commanders as emanating from their respective governments

15. In the unlikely event that any of your immediate subordinates, after making due representations to you, still considers that obedience to your orders would jeopardize the national interests of his country to an extent unjustified by the general situation in the ABDA Area, he has the right, subject to your being immediately notified of such intention, to appeal direct to his own government before carrying out the orders. Such appeals will be made by the most expeditious method, and a copy of the appeal will be communicated simultaneously to you.

16. STAFF AND ASSUMPTION OF COMMAND.-

Your staff will include officers of each of the ABDA powers. You are empowered to communicate immediately with the national commanders in the Area with a view to obtaining staff officers essential to your earliest

U. S. SECRET
BRITISH MOST SECRET

possible assumption of command. Your additional staff requirements will be communicated as soon as possible to the ABDA Governments through channels of communication described in Paragraph 18.

17. You will report when you are in a position effectively to carry out the essential functions of Supreme Command, so that your assumption of command may be promulgated to all concerned.

18. SUPERIOR AUTHORITY.-

As Supreme Commander of the ABDA Area, you will be directly responsible to the ABDA Governments through the agency defined in Annex 2.

Signed

(By Power furnishing
Supreme Commander)

Countersigned:

Other ABDA Representatives.

U. S. SECRET
BRITISH MOST SECRET

ANNEX 1
to
US - ABC-4/5

BOUNDARIES OF ABDA AREA

1. THE ABDA AREA IS BOUNDED AS FOLLOWS:

    On the North: By the boundary between India and Burma, thence eastward along the Chinese frontier and coastline to the latitude of $30°$ North, thence along the parallel of $30°$ North to the meridian of $140°$ East.

                Note: Indo-China and Thailand are not included in this area.

    On the East: By the meridian of $140°$ East from $30°$ North, to the equator, thence east to longitude $141°$ East, thence south to the boundary of Dutch New Guinea on the South Coast, thence east along the Southern New Guinea Coast to the meridian of $143°$ East, then south down this meridian to the coast of Australia.

    On the South: By the northern coast of Australia from the meridian of $143°$ East, westward to the meridian of $114°$ East, thence northwestward to latitude $15°$ South, longitude $92°$ East.

    On the West: By the meridian of $92°$ East

2. Forces assigned to the ABDA and adjacent areas are authorized to extend their operations into other areas as may be required.

U. S. SECRET
BRITISH MOST SECRET

ANNEX 2
to
US - ABC-4/5

January 5, 1942.

HIGHER DIRECTION OF WAR IN THE ABDA AREA

1. On all important military matters, not within the jurisdiction of the Supreme Commander of the ABDA Area, the United States Chiefs of Staff and the representatives in Washington of the British Chiefs of Staff will constitute the agency for developing and submitting recommendations for decision by the President of the United States and by the British Prime Minister and Minister of Defence, on behalf of ABDA Governments. Among the chief matters on which decisions will be required are:

    a. The provision of reinforcements.

    b. A major change in policy.

    c. Departure from the Supreme Commander's directive.

2. This agency will function as follows:

    a. Any proposal coming either from the Supreme Commander or from any of the ABDA Governments will be transmitted to the Chiefs of Staff Committee both in Washington and in London.

    b. The Chiefs of Staff Committee in London having consulted the Dutch Staff, will immediately telegraph to their representatives in Washington to say whether or not they will be telegraphing any opinions.

    c. On receipt of these opinions, the United States Chiefs of Staff and the representatives in Washington of the British Chiefs of Staff will develop and submit their recommendations to the President, and by telegraph to the Prime Minister and Minister of Defence. The Prime Minister will then inform the President whether he is in agreement with these recommendations.

3. Since London has the machinery for consulting the Dominion Governments, and since the Dutch Government is in London, the British Government will be responsible for obtaining their views and agreement to every stage, and for including these in the final telegram to Washington.

U. S. SECRET
BRITISH MOST SECRET

    4. Agreement having been reached between the President and the Prime Minister and Minister of Defence, the orders to the Supreme Commander will be dispatched from Washington in the name of the ABDA Governments and the respective governments will be fully informed.

U. S. SECRET
BRITISH MOST SECRET

U. S. ABC-4/6
BRITISH WW-14   January 13, 1942

UNITED STATES - BRITISH

CHIEFS OF STAFF

APPROVED AS AMENDED

REPORT BY THE UNITED STATES - BRITISH

JOINT PLANNING COMMITTEE

U. S. SERIAL ABC-4/6,   BRITISH SERIAL WW (J.P.C.)6

MOVEMENTS AND PROJECTS IN THE ATLANTIC THEATER -

FIRST HALF OF 1942

U. S. SECRET
BRITISH MOST SECRET

January 13, 1942

U. S. ABC-4/6
BRITISH WW-14

JOINT PLANNING COMMITTEE REPORT

MOVEMENTS AND PROJECTS IN THE ATLANTIC

THEATER - FOR FIRST HALF OF 1942

1. We have carried out a study of the relative importance and interrelation of the various military movements and projects which affect the Atlantic Theater and which may be required to give effect to the agreed Grand Strategy during the first part of 1942, and submit our conclusions below.

MOVEMENTS AND RELIEFS.

ICELAND AND IRELAND

2. We consider that the move of the United States forces into Northern Ireland and the relief of the British Iceland garrison should proceed as expeditiously as possible in order to relieve British Divisions for the replacement of Australian Divisions in the Middle East and to release forces for operations in French North Africa.

3. The movement of United States Army Air Forces to the United Kingdom should proceed as soon as these forces and shipping become available, so as to increase the weight of attack on Germany.

RELIEF OF ARUBA AND CURACAO

4. The relief of Aruba and Curacao, subject to Dutch concurrence, is to be completed before the end of January.

JOINT UNITED STATES - BRITISH OCCUPATION OF FRENCH NORTH AFRICA.

5. We regard this project as of the first strategical importance in the Atlantic area. We do not, however, possess the resources within the period under consideration to force an entry into French North Africa. We cannot, therefore, initiate this operation unless we are reasonably sure of the assumptions upon which the plan is based, which are:

U. S. SECRET
BRITISH MOST SECRET

   <u>a</u> That, due to Spanish resistance, the Germans will require a period of three months before they can mount a land attack from Spain against Morocco;

   <u>b</u> That once the Spanish mainland has been invaded by Germany, our forces will be admitted freely to Spanish Morocco, and that the Spanish there will not attack us; and

   <u>c</u> That French forces will offer only sporadic resistance, if any.

During the period in which we await this opportunity we think that plans and preparations should be completed and that the movements referred to above (Paragraphs 2, 3, 4) should continue.

 6. If we undertake the North Africa operation, it will have the following adverse effects on other projects:

   <u>a</u> Reduction in British troop movements to the Middle East and Far East by 25,000 men.

   <u>b</u> Suspension of major operations against the Canaries, Cape Verdes, and Diego Suarez.

   <u>c</u> Suspension of the relief of British troops in Iceland by United States troops.

   <u>d</u> Reduction in the rate of movement of United States troops to North Ireland.

   <u>e</u> Weakening of British strength in the United Kingdom.

   <u>f</u> Inability to move sizable forces to Northeast Brazil if such action should become necessary.

   <u>g</u> Reduction in the supply of British fighter aircraft to Russia.

   <u>h</u> Serious delay in the despatch of urgently needed United States reinforcements and supplies to Pacific island positions and the Far East, to the Pacific Fleet, and to the outlying island bases.

   <u>i</u> Reduction in Atlantic convoys to the United Kingdom and Russia, due to diversions of shipping and escorts.

  (NOTE: If any of the other operations mentioned in this paper are undertaken, they will adversely affect other operations in some or all of the above ways to a greater or less extent).

U. S. SECRET
BRITISH MOST SECRET

CANARIES AND PORTUGUESE ATLANTIC ISLANDS.

7. A German invasion of Spain will lead to the immediate denial of Gibraltar as a Naval Base and in all probability the involvement of Portugal as well as Spain in the war. In those circumstances, it will be essential to secure the Canaries as a Naval Base. It is possible that the Spaniards would themselves offer us facilities in these islands. On the other hand, the Spaniards may oppose our occupation of the Canaries. While a Spanish offer of facilities would eliminate the need for a large occupying force, it would be necessary to provide sufficient additional air and anti-aircraft defenses to meet the threat of German air forces based on the mainland of Africa, as well as harbor protection for the Naval Base, and for an air patrol of the sea.

8. If we have gained an entry into French North Africa and the Spaniards subsequently acquiesce in a German move into Spain, we could not at the same time undertake an operation to capture the Canaries.

9. If the opportunity to carry out North Africa operations does not occur, and the Germans move into Spain with Spanish acquiescence, the capture of the Canaries, even against opposition, and the occupation of the Azores and Cape Verdes will become essential.

10. It has been agreed that the responsibility for the occupation of the Canaries is a British one, but it would probably be necessary to obtain Naval assistance from the United States. A British assaulting force is already earmarked for this operation and should, we consider, be kept in being.

11. Occupation of the Cape Verdes has been accepted as a United States responsibility. A portion of the United States Army forces set up for North Africa would be used for this operation. The necessary naval support would have to be provided by United States Naval Forces.

12. In the event of a German move into the Iberian Peninsula, it is almost certain that Portugal will admit British forces into the Azores, and probably Madeira. For the security of these islands the chief requirement will be air and anti-aircraft defenses and harbor protection. The provision of these forces is a British responsibility and the necessary forces should be earmarked. Considerable difficulty, however, will be found in providing the shipping for this operation simultaneously with that for North Africa or the Canaries.

13. If the move of British forces to the Azores becomes possible, we are of the opinion that the United States should occupy the Cape Verdes in order to make certain that these islands are denied to the enemy and secured for future use. The occupation of the Cape Verdes will be of considerable

U. S. SECRET
BRITISH MOST SECRET

importance if we do not succeed in gaining entry into French North Africa and are compelled to undertake operations in French West Africa at a later date.

OCCUPATION OF FRENCH WEST AFRICA

14. If we fail to occupy North Africa and Axis occupation appears imminent, then the capture of French West Africa will be essential. If we do not obtain French cooperation in French North Africa, it is unlikely that we shall gain free entry into Dakar. It is therefore necessary to plan the capture of Dakar against opposition. With the joint resources available it is not, in our opinion, possible to undertake an operation of this nature until the late Autumn of 1942 when the weather conditions become favorable. It has been agreed that the United States should be responsible for this operation and we suggest that the planning and training should be put in hand. We propose for consideration that as a preliminary, and simultaneously with the occupation of the Cape Verdes, United States Air and other appropriate forces should be moved to the Freetown - Bathurst area. Their presence in this area will increase the security of the Trans-African Reinforcement Route and the naval base at Freetown.

NORTHEAST BRAZIL

15. The security of Northeast Brazil is of strategic importance as a link in the communications between America and the Trans-African reinforcement route. Germany established in West Africa immediately becomes a threat to the South American Continent, in addition to the threat to Atlantic sea communications. The danger of an Axis-inspired uprising in Brazil, which would interrupt the air route through Africa to the Middle and Far East cannot be disregarded. The operation is a United States responsibility. Plans have been prepared and formations set up for this task.

DIEGO SUAREZ

16. Although the denial of the naval base of Diego Suarez to the enemy is of considerable strategic importance, no British force will be available to undertake this operation within the period under consideration if the force for the Canaries operation is kept in being. Moreover, if this operation were carried out in the near future it might prejudice our chance of obtaining French collaboration in North Africa. We are therefore of the opinion that we can not hold a force ready to undertake this operation at present.

17. We therefore recommend that:

    a The movement of United States Army and Air forces to Iceland, Ireland, and the United Kingdom should proceed as expeditiously as possible.

U. S. SECRET
BRITISH MOST SECRET

    <u>b</u>. That the perfection of a Joint United States - British Plan and preparations for operations in French North Africa should proceed as rapidly as possible.

    <u>c</u>. That under the hypotheses set out in this paper, the United States should prepare plans for:

    (1) The occupation of the Cape Verde Islands both against opposition and by invitation.

    (2) The capture of Dakar against opposition for the Autumn of 1942.

    <u>d</u>. That the United States plan for the security of Northeast Brazil should be kept active.

    <u>e</u>. That under the hypotheses set out in this paper, the British should prepare or perfect plans for:

    (1) The capture of the Canaries.

    (2) The occupation of the Canaries by invitation.

    (3) The occupation of the Azores and Madeira by invitation.

    (4) The capture of Diego Suarez against opposition.

U. S. SECRET
BRITISH MOST SECRET

U. S. SERIAL ABC-4/7   Washington, D. C.
   (APPROVED)
BRITISH SERIAL WW-12   January 11, 1942.

UNITED STATES - BRITISH

CHIEFS OF STAFF

APPROVED

REPORT BY THE UNITED STATES - BRITISH

JOINT PLANNING COMMITTEE

U. S. ABC-4/7   British WW-12

ESTABLISHMENT OF UNITED STATES FORCES IN NORTH IRELAND

U. S. SECRET
BRITISH MOST SECRET

U. S. SERIAL ABC-4/7   Washington, D. C.
BRITISH SERIAL WW (JPC) 7   January 10, 1942.

ESTABLISHMENT OF UNITED STATES FORCES IN NORTH IRELAND

1. MISSION.

United States Army troops will be dispatched to North Ireland for the accomplishment of the following missions:

a   To relieve the mobile elements of the British forces in North Ireland and, in cooperation with British local defense forces, to defend North Ireland against attack by Axis Powers.

b   To be prepared to move into South Ireland for the defense thereof.

2. FORCES.

The forces which will be employed are the V Army Corps, consisting of the 32d, 34th, 37th Divisions, Corps Troops, Army and Corps Service Elements, with the 1st Armored Division attached. This force is under the command of Major General Edmund L. Daley, U. S. Army. The strength of the field forces, less aviation and auxiliary units and anti-aircraft units, is approximately 105,000 officers and men, for which approximately 1,207,500 ship tons are required. The strength of the anti-aircraft personnel (to be provided later) is approximately 31,000 officers and men. The strength of aviation and auxiliary personnel is approximately 22,000 officers and men. Movement of air units can commence on or about February 1, 1942, if shipping is available. When the air and anti-aircraft support is assumed by the United States forces, an additional 583,000 ship tons will be required.

3. COMMAND.

Command of all United States Army forces and personnel in the British Isles, including those in North Ireland, is vested in Major General James E. Chaney, who has been designated, "Commander United States Army Forces in the British Isles." The term "command" is defined as that control of individuals, forces, functions, and establishments which is normally vested in, and exercised by, United States Army commanders by law, regulations, and competent orders. General Chaney is authorized to arrange with appropriate British authorities for the employment:

    (1)   of organizations of his command under British control, and

    (2)   of British organizations under United States control.

U. S. SECRET
BRITISH MOST SECRET

4. STRATEGIC DIRECTION.

<u>a</u> The strategic direction of the United States Army Forces in the British Isles will be exercised by the British Government through the Commander, United States Army Forces in the British Isles.

<u>b</u> The term "strategic direction" is defined to mean the function of prescribing for a force as a whole the general mission which it is to carry out over a long period of time, and such modifications of that general mission as may from time to time become necessary or desirable, without any control of details of tactical operations or administrative matters.

<u>c</u> It is agreed however that units assigned to the United States North Ireland Force will not be moved to areas outside Ireland without prior consent of the Commanding General, Field Forces, United States Army.

5. ARRANGEMENTS FOR THE OPERATION.

The following agreements in respect to arrangements for the operation have been arrived at:

<u>a</u> Questions relative to despatch of United States Army Forces and materials from the United States that may require British collaboration will be handled through the British Mission in the United States.

<u>b</u> Matters connected with command, reception, distribution, accommodation and maintenance of the United States Army Forces in Northern Ireland that may require collaboration between the two governments will be handled for the United States through the Commander, United States Forces in the British Isles.

<u>c</u> WEAPONS AND EQUIPMENT

(1) ANTI-AIRCRAFT. Initially all anti-aircraft protection for United States Field Forces, establishments and installations will be the responsibility of the British. Eventually anti-aircraft protection for United States forces in Northern Ireland will be provided from United States personnel equipped and maintained for armament and ammunition from British sources.

(2) FIELD ARTILLERY. Initially 144 25-pounders, with 1500 rounds per gun, will be delivered by the British to United States Forces in Northern Ireland. The British will supply additional ammunition and maintenance equipment for these weapons as requested by the Commander, United States Forces in the British Isles.

U. S. SECRET
BRITISH MOST SECRET

        (3) AIR. It will be the responsibility of the British to provide appropriate air protection and support for the United States Field Forces, establishments and installations in Northern Ireland, in their mission, until such time as the means are made available to the Commander, United States Forces in the British Isles, to assume this responsibility.

    d   SHELTER.

It will be the responsibility of the British to provide shelter for the United States Army Forces in Northern Ireland.

U. S. SECRET
BRITISH MOST SECRET

U.S. SERIAL ABC-4/8　(APPROVED)　　　　　　　　　　　　　　January 13, 1942.
BRITISH SERIAL WW-13

UNITED STATES - BRITISH

CHIEFS OF STAFF

APPROVED

REPORT BY THE UNITED STATES - BRITISH

JOINT PLANNING COMMITTEE

DEFENSE OF ISLAND BASES

BETWEEN HAWAII AND AUSTRALIA

U. S. SECRET
BRITISH MOST SECRET

U.S. SERIAL ABC-4/8 January 10, 1942.
BRITISH SERIAL WW (J.P.C.)8

JOINT PLANNING COMMITTEE

REPORT FOR THE CHIEFS OF STAFF

COMMITTEE

DEFENSE OF ISLAND BASES

BETWEEN HAWAII AND AUSTRALIA

1. There is under development and approaching completion, an air route suitable for the use of both long and medium range aircraft and extending from Hawaii to Australia. Airdromes are located at Palmyra, Christmas, Canton, American Samoa, Fiji, and New Caledonia. In addition to their use as staging points along the air route, all of these islands are valuable outposts of the defenses of the Hawaiian Islands or of New Zealand and Australia. They will serve also as operating bases for naval and air forces.

2. In addition to its military importance, New Caledonia is an important Japanese objective, since it is the principal readily accessible source of supply for nickel, of which the Japanese have at present only a limited supply. At present the total output of nickel is shipped to the United States. In emergency this source of supply could be denied to the Japanese for some time by the destruction of the blast furnaces, power supply, and limited loading facilities.

3. It is planned also to establish at Borabora, in the Society Islands, which are under Free French jurisdiction, a base for refuelling naval vessels and other shipping en route to and from the Southwest Pacific.

4. The defense of all the island positions along the route, depends ultimately upon their support by naval and air forces. The final strength of forces recommended herein is based on the length of time which in present circumstances may elapse before naval and air support can be made effective. The strength of the forces required will have to be kept under constant review. In the present situation, the Japanese appear to be able to attack New Caledonia or Fiji at an early date with a force of at least one infantry division, supported by strong naval and air forces.

5. The present garrisons of the island bases are inadequate to hold out unsupported against the attacks of which the Japanese are capable. The degree

U. S. SECRET
BRITISH MOST SECRET

of resistance to the Japanese of the French and native troops in New Caledonia is unknown.

6. The United States is able to provide forces for the defense of Palmyra, Christmas, Canton, American Samoa, and Borabora.

7. New Zealand is sending most of the personnel needed for the defense of Viti Levu. The United States already is providing one pursuit squadron and very considerable quantities of the equipment required for the Fijis. The remainder is being supplied from British sources. Most of the equipment needed will be supplied in the near future.

8. Although we consider that New Caledonia should be an Australian responsibility, we are informed that, owing to the scarcity of troops for home defense in the absence of four divisions overseas, Australia is unable to increase the small garrison of one company now in New Caledonia within the next six months. Australia is laying minefields in the approaches to Noumea and Tontouta. We consider that it is important to provide more adequate defenses in the island as early as possible. The only way to do this would be for the United States to send the necessary forces. These would, however, initially be at the expense of the ABDA Area. An opinion should also be obtained from Australia as to the priority for arming the 3700 Free French on the island. A list has been received of their requirements.

RECOMMENDATIONS

9. a. That the United States arrange for the local defense of Palmyra, Christmas, Canton, American Samoa, and Borabora. This is now being accomplished.

b. That the Dominion of New Zealand be responsible for the local defense of the Fiji Islands.

c. That the United States assist in providing equipment and air defenses for the Fiji Islands.

d. That the defense of New Caledonia should in principle be accepted as an Australian responsibility, but that the United States should as a temporary measure, furnish forces as early as possible for the defense of the island, immediately after meeting the emergency in the ABDA Area. The question of arming the Free French troops should be taken up between the United States and British Staffs as soon as an opinion has been obtained from Australia as to the priority.

e. Arrangements should be made immediately by the British with the Free French for the demolition, if necessary, of the furnaces and power plant

U. S. SECRET
BRITISH MOST SECRET

of the nickel mines and the loading facilities for chrome and nickel ore in New Caledonia.

  f. That Australia and New Zealand afford all practicable logistic support to United States forces which may be assigned to assist in the defense of the Fijis and New Caledonia.

  g. The attached table shows forces present in the islands, or en route, and those we recommend should be sent in the future as shipping and naval escorts become available.

U. S. SECRET
BRITISH MOST SECRET

ANNEX TO ABC-4/8

DEFENSE OF ISLAND BASES

BETWEEN HAWAII AND AUSTRALIA

PLACE	DEFENSES NOW THERE OR EN ROUTE	ESTIMATED DESIRABLE GARRISON TO BE COMPLETED AS FORCES, NAVAL ESCORT, AND SHIPPING BECOME AVAILABLE (Includes Col. (b))	REMARKS
(a)	(b)	(c)	(d)
1. NEW CALEDONIA	One Co. A.I.F. Approximately 3,000 Free French Forces (inadequately equipped) 2 6" Fixed Defense Guns (Free French)	Army 1 Inf. Division (4 regiments) 24 Heavy A.A. guns. 48 Light A.A. guns. 24 .50 Calibre A.A. M.G.'s. 12 A.A. Searchlights 8 155 m.m. C.A. guns 1 Eng. Regt. (Gen. Serv.) Air 1 Pursuit Sq. (25 aircraft) 1 Medium Bomb. Sq. (13 aircraft) Air Warning Service. Approximate Total Strength 40,000. See Notes (a) and (b) in Col. (d).	Note (a). Does not include Free French Forces. This island is 230 miles long and 30 miles wide. Force envisages protection of the 3 to 4 air fields, and, in the southern half of the island, the harbor of Noumea. Note (b). The size of the garrison is subject to review as a result of early reconnaissance and degree of assistance afforded by Free French; latter entails completing re-equipment of Free French.

- 1 -

U. S. SECRET
BRITISH MOST SECRET

ANNEX TO ABC-4/8

PLACE	DEFENSES NOW THERE OR EN ROUTE	ESTIMATED DESIRABLE GARRISON TO BE COMPLETED AS FORCES, NAVAL ESCORT, AND SHIPPING BECOME AVAILABLE (Includes Col. (b))	REMARKS
(a)	(b)	(c)	(d)
2. FIJI	Naval 1 Minesweeper 4 Motor Patrol Boats Army 6 New Zealand Inf. Bns. 1 Regular Fiji Bn. (1/8 European) 1 Territorial Fiji Bn. (1/3 European) 28 Field Guns 2 6" C.A. guns at Momi 2 6" C.A. guns at Suva 2 4.7" C.A. guns at Suva 2 60 Pounders 2 6" Howitzers 4 Bofors 4 3" A.A. guns 6 A.A. Searchlights Air 9 Reconnaissance Bombers* 9 Miscellaneous Aircraft* 4 Singapore Flying Boats 700 Men, Air Corps) 25 Airplanes,) U.S. Fighters) 2 sets RADAR	Naval 1 Minesweeper 8 Motor Patrol Boats Army 8 Inf. Bns. 16 Heavy A.A. guns 28 Light A.A. guns 12 .50 Cal. A.A. M.G.'s. 12 A.A. Searchlights 2 C.A. 155 m.m. guns for Momi 4 6" C.A. guns at Momi and Suva 2 4.7" C.A. guns at Suva 2 60 Pounders 2 6" Howitzers 28 Field Guns 1 Co. Tanks (L) (13 Tanks) Air 1 Pursuit (I) Squad. (25 Aircraft) 1 Medium Bombardment Squad. (16 Aircraft) 1 Flying Boat Squad. (8 Aircraft) 4 Sets RADAR	Air U.S. Army is supplying the pursuit squadron. *Obsolete. Should be replaced by Hudsons due to New Zealand under approved allocations.

- 2 -

U. S. SECRET
BRITISH MOST SECRET

ANNEX TO ABC-4/8

PLACE	DEFENSES NOW THERE OR EN ROUTE	ESTIMATED DESIRABLE GARRISON TO BE COMPLETED AS FORCES, NAVAL ESCORT, AND SHIPPING BECOME AVAILABLE (Includes Col.(b))	REMARKS
(a)	(b)	(c)	(d)
3. SAMOA	4 6" guns 18 3" A.A. guns 42 .50 M.G's. 42 .30 M.G's. 415 Marines 150 Samoan Marines 1 Regiment of Marines 12 75 m.m. guns 1 Co. Light Tanks (13 Tanks) Hq. Troops 6 5" guns Total - 5,015 U.S. Marines 6 Scout observation seaplanes (Navy) 2 Sets RADAR	As in column (b) 1 Fighter Squadron (By U. S. Marines) 1 Dive Bomber Squadron	
4. CANTON	45 Engineers 10 Medical and Communication 10 Artillery Personnel 2 75 m.m. guns 12 Machine guns	2 Cos. Inf. Rifle 4 guns C.A. A.A. (90 m.m.) 8 guns C.A. A.A. (37 m.m.) 12 Cal. .50 A.A. M.G's. 2 75 m.m. guns 2 5" Cal. .51 Navy guns 8 37 m.m. A/T guns 2 5" Navy guns 1 Pursuit Squadron (25 Aircraft) 2 RADAR	

U. S. SECRET
BRITISH MOST SECRET

ANNEX TO ABC-4/8

PLACE	DEFENSES NOW THERE OR EN ROUTE	ESTIMATED DESIRABLE GARRISON TO BE COMPLETED AS FORCES, NAVAL ESCORT, AND SHIPPING BECOME AVAILABLE (Includes Col. (b))	REMARKS
(a)	(b)	(c)	(d)
5. CHRISTMAS ISLAND	125 Engineers, Medical and Signal Personnel 10 Artillery Personnel 12 Machine Guns 4 3" A.A. Guns 2 75 m.m. Guns 2 155 m.m. Guns	1 Bn. Inf. 4 guns C.A. A.A. (90 m.m.) 8 guns C.A. A.A. (37 m.m.) 12 Cal. .50 M.G's. A.A. 2 75 m.m. guns 2 5" Cal. .51 Navy guns 5 searchlights 1 Pursuit Sqdn. (25 aircraft) 2 Sets, RADAR	
6. PALMYRA	479 Marines 4 5" guns 4 3" A.A. guns 8 .50 A.A. Machine Guns 8 .30 A.A. Machine Guns 2 Sets, RADAR	As in column (b) 1 Pursuit Squadn. (25 aircraft)	Certain other equipment now installed, details of which are not now available.
7. BORABORA	NONE	1 Inf. Regt. (- 2 Bns.) 12 guns A.A. (90 m.m.) 24 guns A.A. (37 m.m.) 24 Cal. .50 M.G's. 8 guns (75 m.m.) 2 CA Btrys. (Harbor Defense) 6 Scout observation seaplanes (Navy) Services	

U. S. SECRET
BRITISH MOST SECRET

U.S. ABC-4/9   January 10, 1942
BRITISH WW-10

                        UNITED STATES - BRITISH

                           CHIEFS OF STAFF

                           APPROVED REPORT

                                 BY

                UNITED STATES - BRITISH JOINT PLANNING COMMITTEE

                U. S. SERIAL ABC-4/9, BRITISH SERIAL WW(J.P.C.)9

                        IMMEDIATE ASSISTANCE TO CHINA

U. S. SECRET
BRITISH MOST SECRET

U.S. ABC-4/9
BRITISH WW-10

January 10, 1942

JOINT PLANNING COMMITTEE REPORT

TO

CHIEFS OF STAFF

IMMEDIATE ASSISTANCE TO CHINA

1. The United States War Department has been exploring methods of increasing assistance to China so that better effect might be realized from utilization of that country's resources against Japan. Information, currently available, seems to indicate a definite and progressive weakening, morally and materially, in China's war effort. The War Department regards it as of profound importance that such steps as may be practicable and are consistent with other commitments be promptly taken to reverse this trend

2. The chief obstacle to producing a better military result in China, aside from a general scarcity of munitions, is that country's almost complete isolation. Communication with the Generalissimo is difficult and subject to delay and possible interception. The long, poorly maintained, and insecure Burma Road can, at the best, support only a limited truck tonnage, -- while air raids, confusion and lack of coordination at Rangoon further limit the amounts of supplies possible to deliver to the Chinese. Several things are indicated as necessary:

    a. Closer and more effective liaison with the Generalissimo

    b. Increased security for Rangoon and the Burma Road, by air and ground.

    c. Improvement in the control, maintenance, and management of the Burma Road.

    d. Increase in base facilities and technical services.

    e. Increase in Chinese combat strength resulting from above measures.

    f. Close and effective liaison between China and the Commanding General, ABDA Area.

U. S. SECRET
BRITISH MOST SECRET

3. The War Department is considering initiation of the following steps to meet the requirements listed in Paragraph 2:

   a. Arrange with the Generalissimo to accept a United States Army officer of high rank as the United States Representative in China, and to agree to the following as his functions:

   (1) Supervise and control all United States Defense Aid affairs for China.

   (2) Under the Generalissimo, to command all United States forces in China, and such Chinese forces as may be assigned. Should it be necessary for any of these forces to engage in joint operations in Burma, they will come under the command of the Supreme Commander of the ABDA Area, who will issue the necessary directions for the co-operation of the United States Representative's forces with the forces under the British Commanders in Burma.

   (3) Represent the United States Government on any international War Council in China.

   (4) Control and maintain the Burma Road, in China.

   (Note: The following are projected upon the condition that a is, in its entirety, previously accepted by the Generalissimo.)

   b. Dispatch to the South China - Burma area additional aviation strength, initially raising and maintaining the American Volunteer Group at war strength in planes and personnel. In addition, it is considered possible that several Chinese divisions may be quickly equipped for effective combat service in this area, under command of the United States Representative.

   c. Arrange (with the consent of the British) for auxiliary bases in support of the Chinese effort in Burma and India, and provide the technical equipment and troops to assure the efficiency of such Rangoon facilities as are allocated to China, and to assist in the maintenance of the Burma Road.

4. To make this project reasonably effective, British cooperation and agreement are required on the points set forth hereinafter. It is understood that British agreement and cooperation will become effective only in the event that the Generalissimo accords to the United States Representatives the authority implied and indicated in Paragraph 3 a above.

U. S. SECRET
BRITISH MOST SECRET

POINTS ON WHICH BRITISH AGREEMENT IS SOUGHT, UNDER CONDITIONS STATED IN PARAGRAPH 3 a

a. In cooperation with commanders of adjacent areas, the United States Representative to be permitted to establish and/or use bases, routes, and staging areas in India and Burma to support his operations in and north of Burma.

b. The United States Representative to be authorized to make every effort to increase the capacity of the Burma route, throughout its length from Rangoon to Chungking. To do this he will probably be given complete executive control of the China Section of the route. On the British Section, control will still be exercised by the British authorities, both military and civil. To achieve the general aim, these British authorities will be instructed to carry out every possible improvement to the route in accordance with the requirements of the United States Representative and will accept such American technicians and equipment as may be necessary for the improvement of facilities in the Port of Rangoon and along the route itself.

c. The United States Representative, by arrangement with the British Commanders in Burma, to be permitted to construct and/or use necessary airfields in Burma.

d. The United States Representative to be accepted as the principal liaison agency between the Supreme Commander of the ABDA Area and Generalissimo Chiang Kai-shek.

BRITISH MOST SECRET

U.S. ABC-4/CS1
BRITISH WW-1 (FINAL)

December 31, 1941

UNITED STATES - BRITISH

CHIEFS OF STAFF

APPROVED

MEMORANDUM BY THE U. S. AND BRITISH CHIEFS
OF STAFF

AMERICAN - BRITISH

GRAND STRATEGY

Downgraded to *Per JCS m. 43-58 dtd 6-25-58*
U.S. UNCLASSIFIED *British Classification retained*

BRITISH MOST SECRET

U.S. SERIAL ABC-4/CS-1
BRITISH SERIAL W.W.-1 (FINAL)

TO BE KEPT UNDER LOCK AND KEY

It is requested that special care may be taken to ensure the secrecy of this document.

WASHINGTON WAR CONFERENCE

AMERICAN-BRITISH STRATEGY

MEMORANDUM BY THE UNITED STATES AND BRITISH CHIEFS OF STAFF

NOTE: The circulation of this paper should be restricted to the United States and British Chiefs of Staff and their immediate subordinates.

I. GRAND STRATEGY

1. At the A-B* Staff conversations in February, 1941, it was agreed that Germany was the predominant member of the Axis Powers, and consequently the Atlantic and European area was considered to be the decisive theatre.

2. Much has happened since February last, but notwithstanding the entry of Japan into the War, our view remains that Germany is still the prime enemy and her defeat is the key to victory. Once Germany is defeated, the collapse of Italy and the defeat of Japan must follow.

3. In our considered opinion, therefore, it should be a cardinal principle of A-B strategy that only the minimum of force necessary for the safeguarding of vital interests in other theatres should be diverted from operations against Germany.

II. ESSENTIAL FEATURES OF OUR STRATEGY

4. The essential features of the above grand strategy are as follows. Each will be examined in greater detail later in this paper.

    a. The realization of the victory programme of armaments, which first and foremost requires the security of the main areas of war industry.

Note:-
  * For brevity the abbreviated A-B is used to denote American-British

BRITISH MOST SECRET

  b. The maintenance of essential communications.

  c. Closing and tightening the ring around Germany.

  d. Wearing down and undermining German resistance by air bombardment, blockade, subversive activities and propaganda.

  e. The continuous development of offensive action against Germany.

  f. Maintaining only such positions in the Eastern theatre as will safeguard vital interests (see paragraph 18) and denying to Japan access to raw materials vital to her continuous war effort while we are concentrating on the defeat of Germany.

  III. STEPS TO BE TAKEN IN 1942 TO PUT INTO EFFECT THE

ABOVE GENERAL POLICY.

THE SECURITY OF AREAS OF WAR PRODUCTION

 5. In so far as these are likely to be attacked, the main areas of war industry are situated in:-

  a. The United Kingdom.

  b. Continental United States, particularly the West Coast.

  c. Russia.

 6. THE UNITED KINGDOM. - To safeguard the United Kingdom it will be necessary to maintain at all times the minimum forces required to defeat invasion.

 7. THE UNITED STATES. - The main centers of production on or near the West Coast of United States must be protected from Japanese sea-borne attack. This will be facilitated by holding Hawaii and Alaska. We consider that a Japanese invasion of the United States on a large scale is highly improbable, whether Hawaii or Alaska is held or not.

 8. The probable scale of attack and the general nature of the forces required for the defense of the United States are matters for the United States Chiefs of Staff to assess.

 9. RUSSIA. - It will be essential to afford the Russians assistance to enable them to maintain their hold on Leningrad, Moscow, and the oilfields of the Caucasus, and to continue their war effort.

BRITISH MOST SECRET

MAINTENANCE OF COMMUNICATIONS

10. THE MAIN SEA ROUTES WHICH MUST BE SECURED ARE:-

   a. From the United States to the United Kingdom.

   b. From the United States and the United Kingdom to North Russia.

   c. The various routes from the United Kingdom and the United States to Freetown, South America, and the Cape.

   d. The routes in the Indian Ocean to the Red Sea and Persian Gulf, to India and Burma, to the East Indies, and to Australasia.

   e. The route through the Panama Canal, and the United States coastal traffic.

   f. The Pacific routes from the United States and the Panama Canal to Alaska, Hawaii, Australia, and the Far East.

   In addition to the above routes, we shall do everything possible to open up and secure the Mediterranean route.

11. THE MAIN AIR ROUTES WHICH MUST BE SECURED ARE:-

   a. From the United States to South America, Ascension, Freetown, Takoradi, and Cairo.

   b. From the United Kingdom to Gibraltar, Malta and Cairo.

   c. From Cairo to Karachi, Calcutta, China, Malaya, Philippines, Australasia.

   d. From the United States to Australia via Hawaii, Christmas Island, Canton, Palmyra, Samoa, Fiji, New Caledonia.

   e. The routes from Australia to the Philippines and Malaya via the Netherlands East Indies.

   f. From the United States to the United Kingdom via Newfoundland, Canada, Greenland, and Iceland.

   g. From the United States to the United Kingdom via the Azores.

   h. From the United States to Vladivostok, via Alaska.

BRITISH MOST SECRET

12. THE SECURITY OF THESE ROUTES INVOLVES:-

    a. Well-balanced A - B naval and air dispositions.

    b. Holding and capturing essential sea and air bases.

CLOSING AND TIGHTENING THE RING AROUND GERMANY

13. This ring may be defined as a line running roughly as follows: ARCHANGEL - BLACK SEA - ANATOLIA - THE NORTHERN SEABOARD OF THE MEDITERRANEAN - THE WESTERN SEABOARD OF EUROPE.

The main object will be to strengthen this ring, and close the gaps in it, by sustaining the Russian front, by arming and supporting Turkey, by increasing our strength in the Middle East, and by gaining possession of the whole North African coast.

14. If this ring can be closed, the blockade of Germany and Italy will be complete, and German eruptions, e.g. towards the Persian Gulf, or to the Atlantic seaboard of Africa, will be prevented. Furthermore, the seizing of the North African coast may open the Mediterranean to convoys, thus enormously shortening the route to the Middle East and saving considerable tonnage now employed in the long haul around the Cape.

THE UNDERMINING AND WEARING DOWN OF THE GERMAN RESISTANCE

15. In 1942 the main methods of wearing down Germany's resistance will be:-

    a. Ever-increasing air bombardment by British and American Forces.

    b. Assistance to Russia's offensive by all available means.

    c. The blockade.

    d. The maintenance of the spirit of revolt in the occupied countries, and the organization of subversive movements.

DEVELOPMENT OF LAND OFFENSIVES ON THE CONTINENT

16. It does not seem likely that in 1942 any large scale land offensive against Germany except on the Russian front will be possible. We must, however, be ready to take advantage of any opening that may result from the wearing down process referred to in paragraph 15 to conduct limited land offensives.

BRITISH MOST SECRET

17. In 1943 the way may be clear for a return to the Continent, across the Mediterranean, from Turkey into the Balkans, or by landings in Western Europe. Such operations will be the prelude to the final assault on Germany itself, and the scope of the victory program should be such as to provide means by which they can be carried out.

THE SAFEGUARDING OF VITAL INTERESTS IN THE EASTERN THEATRE

18. The security of Australia, New Zealand, and India must be maintained, and the Chinese war effort supported. Secondly, points of vantage from which an offensive against Japan can eventually be developed must be secured. Our immediate object must therefore be to hold:-

    a. Hawaii and Alaska.

    b. Singapore, the East Indies Barrier, and the Philippines.

    c. Rangoon and the route to China.

    d. The Maritime Provinces of Siberia.

The minimum forces required to hold the above will have to be a matter of mutual discussion.

U.S. SECRET
BRITISH MOST SECRET

U.S. ABC-4/CS-3
BRITISH WW-9 (REVISED)   January 10, 1942

UNITED STATES - BRITISH

CHIEFS OF STAFF

APPROVED AS AMENDED - BRITISH CHIEFS OF STAFF

MEMORANDUM

PROCEDURE FOR ASSUMPTION OF COMMAND BY

GENERAL WAVELL

BRITISH MOST SECRET

U.S. ABC-4 C/S 3
BRITISH WW-9 (REVISED)

January 10, 1942.

It is requested that special
care may be taken to insure
the secrecy of this document.

WASHINGTON WAR CONFERENCE

PROCEDURE FOR ASSUMPTION OF COMMAND BY GENERAL WAVELL

Memorandum by British Chiefs of Staff.

1. General Wavell was informed on 29th December, 1941, by the Prime Minister that he was to be the Supreme Commander in the ABDA Area. He was told that his directive would be given to him shortly and that any observations which he might wish to make on its terms would be considered.

2. When the directive was finally approved by the President and the Prime Minister, orders were sent to London (2nd January) that it should be telegraphed to General Wavell immediately - copies were also to be sent to General Pownall and all other British Commanders concerned.

3. At the same time the terms of the directive were communicated to the Dutch, Australian, and New Zealand Governments.

4. The Dutch Government has suggested certain amendments to Annex (ii) to the directive, and these are still under discussion. It is not known whether they have communicated the directive to the Dutch Commanders in the ABDA Area.

5. The Australian Government has put forward views and opinions about the whole arrangement, and have not yet notified their agreement with the directive. It is presumed that they have not yet informed any of their Commanders.

6. The New Zealand Government is only indirectly concerned. There has been no comment on the directive from them.

7. On 2nd January General Wavell was told that much importance was attached to his taking over as soon as possible, and he was asked to specify the earliest date on which he would be ready to assume command. He is now at Singapore, but is expected to be in Batavia today, 10th January. No observations have yet been received from him about his directive, nor has he yet specified a date for assuming command.

U. S. SECRET
BRITISH MOST SECRET

8. Neither the Dutch nor the Australian Government has yet agreed to the directive, though their objections are mainly to the machinery of control laid down in Annex (ii) rather than to the directive itself. The discussions which are proceeding with those Governments may of course be successfully concluded before it becomes necessary to promulgate the date of General Wavell's appointment; but even if they are not, we do not think there need be any delay on that account. We suggest that General Wavell's appointment should be promulgated as soon as he reports he is ready, and that he should then be instructed to carry on, pending the final confirmation of his directive.

9. We accordingly propose that the following action should be taken as soon as General Wavell reports the date on which he will be ready to assume command:-

    a. His Majesty's Government should make a communication in the terms of Annex A to the Governments of the United States, The Netherlands, Australia, New Zealand, India, and China.

    b. His Majesty's Government in the United Kingdom should telegraph to General Wavell in the terms of Annex B.

    c. On receipt of the communication mentioned in a above, the Governments of the United States, The Netherlands, and Australia should at once notify their local Commanders of the date of the assumption of command by General Wavell, and should give any necessary consequential instructions so that the system planned for the ABDA Area can become effective.

    d. The terms of the directive for General Wavell, including Annex (ii), should be settled as soon as possible, and the outcome notified to all concerned.

10. We propose to telegraph home in the terms of Annex C to secure the assent of the Dutch and Australian Governments to this procedure.

                                               (Signed) DUDLEY POUND.
                                                        J. G. DILL.
                                                        C. PORTAL.

Washington, D. C.

    January 10, 1942.

U. S. SECRET
BRITISH MOST SECRET

ANNEX "A"

Draft communication from His Majesty's Government in the United Kingdom to the Governments of the United States, The Netherlands, Australia, New Zealand, China, and India:

Instructions are being sent today to General Wavell that he should assume command of the ABDA Area as from January _____.

Pending final agreement between the Governments concerned on the terms of his directive and on the machinery for the higher direction of war in the ABDA Area, (Annex II to the Directive), General Wavell is being instructed to proceed in accordance with the directive as at present drafted and to communicate with Washington and London as laid down in Paragraph 18 thereof.

Please inform all Commanders concerned, accordingly.

ANNEX "B"

Draft telegram from His Majesty's Government in the United Kingdom to General Wavell:

You are to assume supreme command in the ABDA Area on January _____.

Pending final agreement between the Governments concerned on your directive, you should act in accordance with the directive sent to you in Telegram No. ____, and you should address communications to superior authority in accordance with Paragraph 18 thereof.

General Brett and Admiral Hart are being ordered by the United States Government to report to you as Deputy Supreme Commander and Commander of Combined Naval Forces, respectively, in the ABDA Area.

Governments concerned are notifying their Commanders accordingly.

U. S. SECRET
BRITISH MOST SECRET

ANNEX "C"

Draft telegram from British Chiefs of Staff to Chiefs of Staff Committee, London:

Please put following to Lord Privy Seal:

It is of highest importance that General Wavell should exercise supreme command without delay, as soon as he reports himself ready to do so.

Please propose to Dutch and Australian Governments that as soon as General Wavell reports himself as ready he should be authorized to assume command, pending the acceptance by those Governments of the ABDA machinery as set out in Annex II of his directive.

United States Chiefs of Staff agree.

U. S. SECRET
BRITISH MOST SECRET

U. S. ABC-4/CS4
BRITISH WW-16

January 14, 1942

UNITED STATES - BRITISH

CHIEFS OF STAFF

APPROVED AS AMENDED - UNITED STATES CHIEFS OF STAFF

MEMORANDUM

POST-ARCADIA COLLABORATION

U. S. SECRET
BRITISH MOST SECRET

U. S. ABC-4/CS4   January 14, 1942
BRITISH WW-16

WASHINGTON WAR CONFERENCE

POST-ARCADIA COLLABORATION

MEMORANDUM BY COMBINED CHIEFS OF STAFF

1. In order to provide for the continuance of the necessary machinery to effect collaboration between the United Nations after the departure from Washington of the British Chiefs of Staff, the Combined Chiefs of Staff (formerly designated as "Joint Chiefs of Staff") propose the broad principles and basic organization herein outlined.

2. To avoid confusion we suggest that hereafter the word "Joint" be applied to Inter-Service collaboration of ONE NATION, and the word "Combined" to collaboration between two or more of the UNITED NATIONS.

3. DEFINITIONS. -

    a. The term "Combined Chiefs of Staff" is defined as the British Chiefs of Staff (or in their absence from Washington, their duly accredited representatives), and the United States opposite numbers of the British Chiefs of Staff.

    b. The term "Combined Staff Planners" is defined as the body of officers duly appointed by the Combined Chiefs of Staff to make such studies, draft such plans, and perform such other work as may from time to time be placed on the "Combined Chiefs of Staff Agenda" by that Body, and duly delegated by them to the Combined Staff Planners.

    c. The "Combined Secretariat" is defined as the body of officers duly appointed by the Combined Chiefs of Staff to maintain necessary records, prepare and distribute essential papers, and perform such other work as is delegated to them by the Combined Chiefs of Staff.

4. PERSONNEL. -

    a. The Heads of the Joint Staff Mission, Admiral Sir Charles Little, Lt. General Sir Colville Wemyss, and Air Marshal A. T. Harris, will represent the British Chiefs of Staff in Washington.

    b. The Joint Staff Planners will be:

U. S. SECRET
BRITISH MOST SECRET

    (1) FOR THE BRITISH (for the time being):

      Captain C. E. Lambe, R.N.
      Lt. Col. G. K. Bourne, British Army
      Group Captain S. C. Strafford, R.A.F.

    (2) FOR THE UNITED STATES, the principal members are:

      Rear Admiral R. K. Turner, U.S. Navy
      Brig. Gen. L. T. Gerow, U.S. Army
      Capt. R. E. Davison, U.S. Navy
      Col. E. L. Naiden, U.S. Army

  c. COMBINED SECRETARIAT

  The British members of the Combined Secretariat will be headed by Brigadier Dykes. The United States members will be headed by Commander L. R. McDowell, U.S. Navy.

5. THE COMBINED CHIEFS OF STAFF shall develop and submit recommendations as follows:

  a. For the ABDA Area, specifically as set forth in the Directive, Annex 2 to U.S. ABC-4/5, British WW-6, dated January 5, 1942.

  b. For other areas in which the United Nations may decide to act in concert, along the same general lines as in *a* above, modified as necessary to meet the particular circumstances.

6. THE COMBINED CHIEFS OF STAFF shall accordingly:

  a. Recommend the broad program of requirements based on strategic considerations.

  b. Submit general directives as to the policy governing the distribution of available weapons of war. (It is agreed that finished war equipment shall be allocated in accordance with strategical needs; to effectuate this principle, we recommend the utilization of appropriate bodies in London and Washington, under the authority of the Combined Chiefs of Staff).

  c. Settle the broad issues of priority of overseas military movements.

U. S. SECRET
BRITISH MOST SECRET

    7.   The question of the production and dissemination of complete Military Intelligence to serve the Combined Chiefs of Staff and Combined Staff Planners has been referred to the latter body for a report. Here also, it is contemplated that existing machinery will be largely continued.

    8.   It is planned that the Combined Chiefs of Staff will meet weekly, or more often if necessary; an agenda will be circulated before each meeting.